**Making
Washington
Work for You**

Making Washington Work for You

August Bequai

LexingtonBooks
D.C. Heath and Company
Lexington, Massachusetts
Toronto

Library of Congress Cataloging in Publication Data
Bequai, August.

Making Washington work for you.

Includes index.
1. Administrative agencies—United States—Handbooks,
manuals, etc.   2. Independent regulatory commissions—
United States—Handbooks, manuals, etc.   3. Government
information—United States—Handbooks, manuals, etc.
I. Title.
JK464 1984   353'.0002'02   82–48602
ISBN 0–669–06347–9
ISBN 0–669–06348–7 (pbk.)

Published simultaneously in Canada

Printed in the United States of America

Casebound International Standard Book Number: 0–669–06347–9

Paperback International Standard Book Number: 0–669–06348–7

Library of Congress Catalog Card Number: 82–48602

For my mother and father

For my mother and father

For my mother and father

Contents

Contents

Figures

Acknowledgments

In writing this book I would like to thank my many friends and associates for their assistance and support. I would like to express my special appreciation to Marian P. Dettor for her invaluable typing, editing, comments, and patience.

Introduction

In 1802 the headquarters staff of the U.S. Department of State numbered fewer than a dozen men and women. The federal judiciary employed thirty-six district judges and the U.S. Mint was manned by a workforce of thirteen. The United States was small and rural.

By the turn of the century, the United States had become a global political and economic power. With the new status also came changes in the federal bureaucracy. The 1930s witnessed the New Deal, and Washington, D.C., has never since been the same. The economic, political, and social forces that galvanized the U.S. social fiber also gave rise to the present bureaucratic edifice.

The federal bureaucracy peaked at 3.4 million men and women during World War II. By 1947 it had declined to 2 million. President Johnson's New Society, however, gave it new impetus. The bureaucracy grew; by 1967 it numbered some 3 million, and it has changed little since then.

The federal government presently regulates much of the way we live, eat, vote, breathe, learn, travel, and many other facets of our daily lives. The Founding Fathers, in their wildest dreams, would have never envisioned the present gargantuan federal edifice; like a hydra, it spawns new heads daily.

The growth of the federal establishment, however, is no accident. It thrives on the fears and expectations of the many diverse constituencies that form the United States. It constitutes a response to both perceived and real needs. It is the outcome of political pressures placed on Congress and the executive branch.

This dramatic growth has also sparked opposition. There are many who fear that the federal bureaucracy has supplanted our elected officials. There are those who have come to view the federal bureaucracy as an oppressive force.

In part, these feelings are borne out of frustration: not understanding how the federal agencies that rule our daily lives operate. Few U.S. citizens understand how the Congress, the executive branch, or the faceless federal judiciary work. The more fortunate and affluent sectors of our society have retained the services of private lawyers, lobbyists, and consultants to help them deal with the federal bureaucracy. Thus, the affluent have left it to the experts; the rest of us have resigned ourselves to a state of impotence.

In a democracy it is imperative that the citizenry understand how its bureaucracy operates. The public should have some input, even if limited, in the governance process. This can often be achieved by simply dialing the right telephone number, or addressing your letter to the proper agency. Further, there are ample federal laws that, if employed correctly, give the public access to the records and decision-making process of the federal bureaucracy.

The purpose of this book is to both educate and dispel much of the myth that surrounds the political world of Washington. The book should prove to be a valuable tool for a broad range of individuals; for example the average citizen who needs to better understand how to make his voice heard in the halls of Congress and the federal bureaucracy, the business-person who needs to understand the nuts and bolts of the regulatory process, the government bureaucrat who needs a reference to the federal regulators, or the law clerk/paralegal who needs a time-saving device.

This book offers information on how to achieve the following:

Obtain needed information quickly and inexpensively.

Have an input in the federal decision-making process (presently monopolized by vocal and well-funded pressure groups).

Monitor legislation, rules, and regulations.

Deal with the press corps.

Use the Freedom of Information Act (FOIA) to open up the bureaucracy.

Employ the Privacy Act to safeguard individual privacy.

Handle a government investigation.

Deal with the Internal Revenue Service (IRS).

The book is not a technical encyclopedia on federal regulation. It is an analysis of the inner workings of the federal regulatory maze, Congress and its committees, the executive establishment, and the federal court system.

Washington has been described as Hollywood East; a city where reality is distorted by fantasy. In clear and simple language, this book seeks to open the federal regulatory processes to the outsider. It should prove of value and interest to any person who wants or needs to better understand how Washington works.

**Part I
Opening the Doors**

1 Opening up Washington Can Be Easy

The president of a small New Jersey construction company had read that one of his large competitors had been investigated by the Antitrust Division of the U.S. Department of Justice; the investigation had lasted more than three years, but had not resulted in any formal action. In an effort to discover whether the investigators had uncovered some evidence of price fixing, he filed a Freedom of Information Act (5 U.S.C. 552) (FOIA) request. Soon afterward, he reached a compromise with attorneys for the department who agreed to allow him to review at no cost some 20,000 pages of documents at their Washington offices.

The FOIA has become an important tool with which the average citizen can open up the files of Washington's bureaucracy. An entire industry has sprung up around the act. Some companies now publish FOIA newsletters; others employ large staffs to compile weekly lists of FOIA requests. An army of Washington lawyers has turned the act into a multimillion-dollar annual business.

The FOIA, however, was designed with simplicity in mind; it is an easy tool to employ. In fact, one need not be a lawyer to use it; of the more than 100,000 FOIA requests per year, the majority are placed by laypersons.

The act covers all federal executive departments and also the independent regulatory agencies. (Use of the term *agency* in this chapter applies to all of these entities.) To use the act you need only follow a few guidelines. First, be specific as to what you request; second, know to whom to address your request; and third, know how to draft your request. The objective of this chapter is to instruct you on these guidelines and on how to force the bureaucracy to comply with your request.

Understanding the FOIA

The FOIA was enacted to make the federal bureaucracy more responsive to the public. It applies, however, only to the federal executive bureaucracy; Congress and the federal judiciary are exempt. The FOIA directs the bureaucrats to make available upon request many of their records to any member of the public who requests them; unlike other federal laws

3

that limit access to records to those individuals who are properly and directly concerned.

The federal courts have expanded the FOIA to permit even foreign governments and nationals to employ it. The Mexican government has been permitted to use it to gain access to federal agency records. Corporations have also made use of the act to gain access to the financial records of their competitors. The news media has used it with great success to gain access to touchy political files; and litigants have used it as a vehicle for discovery. Under the act, a requester need not disclose the reason for seeking the information, nor does he have to demonstrate that the public interest will be advanced by the release of the information.

The FOIA itself does not define an *agency record;* this has been left to the federal courts. Some judges have interpreted an agency record to be anything which is written or transcribed and is in the possession of the government. (By that it means one of the federal executive agencies. The FOIA does not apply to local/state governments, though some of these have enacted similar legislation.) Some courts have even gone so far as to define motion pictures as being records.

The applicability of the act, however, depends in part on whether a government agency has or exerts control over the records that have been requested. An agency cannot evade the provisions of the FOIA by physically transferring documents to another agency or other third party. Records and documents filed with an executive department or independent regulatory agency may be subject to release under the act, unless the government demonstrates that they fall under one or more of the nine exemptions to the act.

Thus, a corporation, university, government, or individual that files records with a federal agency, runs the risk of having those records released to any person, corporation, or government that places an FOIA request. The act, however, does not cover the entire bureaucratic maze. The federal courts, the Congress and its committees, as well as the Government Accounting Office (GAO) are not covered. In addition, the act does not cover state and local courts; the government of the District of Columbia or of any U.S. territory; court martials; military commissions; or military authority exercised in time of war. The act, however, does cover all executive departments; independent regulatory agencies; military departments; government-owned corporations; quasi-public corporations; and the executive office of the president.

There is a simple test you can use to determine whether a federal agency falls under the jurisdiction of the act. First, determine whether the agency in question is part of the executive branch of government; second, find out if the agency was established under a specific federal law; and third, inquire whether its daily operations are subject to federal control. If the agency meets all of these, then it probably falls under the scope of the FOIA.

Disclosure Requirements

The FOIA outlines three methods that must be employed by every agency subject to it in making its records available to the public:

1. An agency must publish specifically designated material in the *Federal Register*
2. An agency must make specified material available for inspection and copying
3. Any records not open to disclosure by the first two methods must be made available for inspection and copying at any time an individual places a request.

If any agency fails to comply with the disclosure methods, it must then note its reasons for refusing. The FOIA empowers the federal courts to compel an agency to produce any records it improperly withholds.

The act requires that agencies publish both the locations and the methods by which members of the public may gain access to their records. Agencies are also required to make public their decisions and decision-making procedures, their rules, and the contents of any reports or examinations prepared by their staffs.

According to the act federal agencies must also publish all their general policy statements, interpretations of policy, agency opinions, and all amendments and revisions of their rules. Agencies are further required to make public any administrative staff manual that affects members of the public, provided that the manual does not contain law-enforcement-connected information. The agency bears the burden of demonstrating that release or publication of a manual would impede its law-enforcement functions or efforts.

FOIA Exemptions

The act lists nine categories of records that are exempt from disclosure under its provisions. An agency may thus deny access to its records if these fall under one or more of the following nine exemptions.

1. Records classified (under executive order) as secret for purposes of national defense and foreign policy.

2. Records relating solely to internal personnel rules and practices.
3. All information exempt under other statutes. This applies to such records as income tax returns, which are exempt from disclosure because of IRS prohibitions.
4. Trade secrets and other confidential and corporate information where the release of the records would have an adverse impact on the competitiveness of the provider.
5. Interagency and intraagency memos. These are deemed confidential.
6. Personal information and personnel or medical data where disclosure would constitute an invasion of privacy.
7. Investigatory records compiled for law-enforcement purposes where the release could interfere with legitimate law-enforcement objectives, expose confidential sources to danger, result in an invasion of personal privacy, or expose investigative techniques.
8. Information related to reports on financial institutions, such as files of the Federal Reserve Board pertaining to investigations involving member banks.
9. Geological and geophysical data. This exempts information concerning wells and some maps.

Save for the exemptions, a requester has great latitude in what he can request from an agency. It is the agency that must demonstrate that the records it has withheld fall under one or more of these exemptions. A requesting party has little to lose by placing a request, and then leaving the decision up to the agency.

The federal courts have demonstrated a reluctance to permit agencies to withhold information; they tend to side with the public. As a result, many agencies will work out a compromise if they are convinced that you are prepared to go to court for relief. Since many of the agencies do not handle their own FOIA-related litigation—this is handled by the Department of Justice (DOJ)—they may find themselves pressured by DOJ attorneys to reach a compromise. DOJ attorneys are primarily concerned with more serious litigation and will prove receptive to compromise.

How to Request and Appeal

You often do not need the expensive services of a Washington law firm to handle an FOIA request for you. Anyone who can write a letter can easily do it himself by following some simple guidelines. Although some agencies will process a verbal FOIA request, it is better to place your request in letter form (see figure 1–1). Should the request be denied

(Date) _____

Freedom of Information Officer
(Name and address of agency)

RE: Freedom of Information Request

Dear Sir:

Pursuant to 5 U.S.C. 552, I request your office to make available to me for inspection and copying all letters, memoranda, reports and documents of any kind that relate to (specify in detail your request).

Very truly yours,
(Signature and name of requesting party)

Figure 1–1. Sample FOIA Request Letter

(either in whole or part) and you decide to appeal, you will be required to present documentary evidence regarding the date, place, and records you requested.

Your request should be as specific as possible about the records you seek; further, both in your letter and envelope be sure to designate your inquiry as an *FOIA Request*. If you fail to do so, the request may end up with the wrong official. Anyone who has had any dealings with the federal bureaucracy will tell you that it is not difficult for correspondence to become lost in an agency's bureaucratic maze.

Once an agency receives an FOIA request, it has up to ten working days to respond. If an agency cannot comply with the time requirement (few federal agencies will respond within ten days) it can request a ten-day extension. The act provides for additional extensions upon application to the federal courts. Thus, be prepared for extensive delays on your FOIA request.

Federal agencies are inundated with thousands of requests that fail to adequately describe the records requested; this can also result in delays. In some cases, the records sought may be located in one of the agency's field offices. If you know the field office in which the records you seek are located, be sure to indicate this in your request. Specificity about the records sought and their location can help to save time and also facilitate compliance by the agency. If you have an exceptional or urgent need for the records requested, indicate this in your letter to the FOIA officer. This can sometimes expedite a request. As a general rule, the bureaucrats do not look fondly on the FOIA; if you provide them with an excuse for delaying your request, they will do so.

If an agency wholly or partially denies your FOIA request (which is normal), it must then set out the reasons for its denial. The agency's FOIA office must also advise you that you have thirty days to appeal its denial, and it must list the name(s) and title(s) of the person(s) who denied your request.

When denying a request, the agency will list one or more of the nine FOIA exemptions. If the records you requested are not in the agency's possession, this also can serve as basis for a denial. The agency is not obligated to forward your request to another agency.

If an agency refuses to provide you with either all or some of the records you requested on the grounds that these are exempt materials, you have a right under the act to appeal its refusal. The act does not require the agency to provide you with a periodic update on the documents it has already released, nor on those that have come into its possession since your request. The agency is also not obligated to provide you with an update on documents it has released to you; for this information you may have to file an additional FOIA request.

FOIA appeals are administrative in nature; agency regulations are specific as to the procedures and time framework for an appeal. The requesting party has thirty days to appeal an agency's decision. Once an appeal is filed, the agency then has up to twenty working days (after receipt of the appeal) to decide on the merits of the request.

When an agency fails to comply with the time limitations imposed on it by the act (either at the request or appeal stage), a requesting party has exhausted the administrative remedies; he can choose to go to court to seek injunctive relief. However, this route (although the most direct) can sometimes be expensive; thus, unless there is an urgent need for the records in question, it is better to first exhaust all internal remedies. If the agency continues to stick by its original decision or fails to act within twenty working days, you can seek relief in federal court.

Unless an appeal is frivolous, most agencies will compromise; they will usually provide some of the records you requested. The appellate source will often reverse the decision of the FOIA office. You stand to lose nothing by appealing an adverse decision. Appeals should always be in writing and should be addressed to the appropriate agency sources (see figure 1–2). The agency's regulations will detail the procedures you should follow. In addition, note on your letter and envelope that this is

(Date) _____

Director of (name of agency)
(Name and address of agency)

RE: Freedom of Information Appeal

Dear Sir:

This is an appeal from the denial of my Freedom of Information Act request for records as indicated in the attached letter. This request was denied under Exemption _____ of the act.

I believe that this denial was not correct, and does not fall under the scope of Exemption _____ of the act. (State, in a paragraph or two, why you do not feel they fall within the exemption cited by the agency).

Since the records in issue therefore are not exempted from disclosure under exemption of the act, they should be made available to me or any of my agents for review and copying.

Very truly yours,
(Signature and name of requesting party)

Figure 1–2. Sample FOIA Appeal Letter

an FOIA appeal. Be sure to attach copies of the agency's denial letter; also detail why you feel that the FOIA office erred in denying your request.

The act does allow agencies to charge the public a fee for their services; but the fee must be a reasonable standard charge for the direct costs of searching and copying the requested documents. However, unless the costs are excessive, many of the agencies will not charge a fee.

A requesting party can avoid paying all or part of the fee if: he is indigent; the public in general would benefit from the release of the records sought; he is willing to examine the records at the agency's offices rather than be provided with photocopies; or he has specified a dollar-amount ceiling on the costs.

Agencies have great latitude when deciding whether to waive their fees, although the courts do require that their decisions be made in good faith. An agency cannot charge a fee for time spent on examining the records in question for the purpose of determining if they are exempt; time spent in deleting exempt information from the records; or time spent in preparing the records for inspection by the requesting party. In most cases, an agency will charge only a nominal fee. If you inspect the records at its offices, you can avoid paying the costs altogether.

In dealing with the FOIA office, it is recommended that you be courteous; avoid being combative. Time is of the essence in FOIA litigation, and time is on the side of the bureaucrats. If the FOIA office fails to comply altogether with your request, you will find that the courts are open for relief; they can also award attorney's fees and court costs.

Whenever possible seek out the diplomatic route. Do not hesitate to write a thank-you letter to the staff; especially to their superiors. If there are any delays on your request, try the telephone and make polite inquiries. Be firm when necessary, but not argumentative. There are times when the soft approach is extremely effective.

Every FOIA officer knows that you have the right to seek judicial relief; there is no need to remind him of this in your communications. If diplomacy fails, then assert your rights and take a tough stance. However, because you may have to deal with the agency's FOIA office again, it does not pay to alienate an officer. You need to strike a balance; the act details your rights, and our courts have jurisdiction to enforce them when necessary. However, it is the bureaucracy that collects and stores the records; it knows how to play the game.

Handling the Litigation

U.S. district courts are empowered to enjoin a federal agency from withholding its records; they can order it to produce any and all documents it has improperly withheld. Many of the courts take the position that unless the records are covered by one or more of the nine FOIA exemptions, they should be made available to the public upon request. The burden is on the agency to demonstrate that the records fall within the exemptions. A requesting party need not give any reason why he seeks access to the agency's records. The party need only inform the court that he has made a formal FOIA request for the records; that the request was denied by the agency; and that he now seeks relief from the court.

A party that brings a court action can also request the court to order the agency to pay his attorney's fees and court costs. If he prevails in the litigation, most courts will order an agency to pay some or all of the legal expenditures incurred by the requesting party to enforce the FOIA. Some courts, however, have started granting fees and court costs to the government in those cases where a party brings a frivolous lawsuit.

As regards an FOIA lawsuit, a plaintiff (requesting party) can bring an action in any one of the following four forums.

1. The district in which the plaintiff resides
2. The district in which the plaintiff has his principal place of business
3. The district in which the agency's records are located
4. The District of Columbia

The act also provides that FOIA litigation "takes precedence on the [court's] docket over all cases and shall be assigned for hearing and trial or for argument at the earliest practicable date and expedited in every way." However, because of the growth in FOIA litigation, few courts pay much heed to this provision. FOIA litigation can be time-consuming and costly.

During an FOIA trial, the court can review (de novo) the agency's decision; this is one of the reasons why it is imperative that you make all of your requests in writing and also keep a detailed record of all your communications with the agency's FOIA office. The court can choose to review the records at issue, consider affidavits by the agency's officials, and also hear testimony. A court may even review the entire case before rendering its decision.

At the trial level, it is not enough for an agency to allege that the records in question are confidential; it must convince the court with facts. The agency, however, can request that the judge sitting on the case review the records in the privacy of his chamber; this is especially common in the intelligence community. These private inspections are discretionary with the court, which also has discretion regarding which documents it will inspect.

A party may request a court to order an agency to prepare a detailed statement about the records in its possession. This request is known as a Vaughn Statement; to obtain such a statement, a party must first file a Vaughn Motion. The agency's statement must be as detailed as possible, without actually revealing confidential information. If an agency is ordered by the court to file such a statement, it must list and describe in detail all of the records it has withheld, and provide a detailed justification for why it has decided to withhold the records. The final decision, however, rests with the court; it can refuse a party's request for such a detailed statement.

Reverse Litigation

A reverse-FOIA lawsuit is an action taken to prevent a federal agency from disclosing information made available to it by a private source. The basis for such lawsuits is that the records are confidential and were supplied to the agency with that understanding, and the agency erred in its decision to release them.

An individual or corporation may argue that the records it provided the agency are, for example, personal records, trade secrets, or other confidential information, and thus exempt from FOIA disclosure. A party that opposes disclosure may also argue that the release of such records constitutes a violation of privacy, and is thus prohibited under the Privacy Act or some other federal statute.

As the FOIA has increasingly become a discovery vehicle for corporations, reverse-FOIA litigation has kept pace. It is often employed by corporations to safeguard business records that they have filed with an agency. The objective is to prevent a competitor access to such information.

The FOIA is a disclosure statute; it makes no provision for giving third parties a voice in an agency's decision to make disclosure. It does require an agency to notify a third party of its decision. To ensure that an agency will provide you with timely notice, you should submit along with any records a written statement requesting that its staff notify you promptly in the event that these records are considered for disclosure. Such a statement will not guarantee that you will be notified; it does, however, provide minimal safeguard.

A reverse-FOIA lawsuit can be brought in the district in which the records are stored; the district in which the agency is located; the district in which the corporation or individual resides or does business; or the District of Columbia. For purposes of venue, the proper forum is the one in which all the defendants reside, in which the claim arose, or in which the party bringing the action resides.

Individuals and corporations have employed the FOIA effectively to gain access to valuable information. Attorneys have used it to gain access to agency records that may be of import to their clients. Consumers have used it to uncover abuses in government. The FOIA was designed to be a simple tool that the average person can employ with ease.

You do not need the services of attorneys to file an FOIA request or to handle an administrative appeal. FOIA litigation, however, should be handled by counsel. In addition, use of counsel may be valuable in placing an FOIA request in the event that you choose not to be identified. The FOIA is an effective tool when used properly; if abused, it can prove to be self-defeating.

Appendix 1A
Analysis of FOIA
Litigation

The act requires disclosure of government records to any person except as specifically stated in the nine exemptions and elsewhere as required by statute.

I   Reverse FOIA Litigation: attempts to limit an agency's discretionary power.

    A. FOIA itself does not provide for the furnishers of information to the government to go to court to prevent disclosure of their information. However, the furnishers of information have been allowed by the courts to seek review of an agency's decision to disclose; also, agency regulations have provisions allowing suppliers of information notice of third party requests for information and an opportunity to challenge.

    B. Reasons for reverse suits: because suppliers are unable to predict treatment of information; there is a real possibility of disclosure to third parties by the agency. Some agencies notify interested parties of FOIA request and set forth procedures for challenges, others do not have such procedures.

    C. Promises of confidentialilty: by agency to supplier not withholding.

II.   What Triggers Litigation

    A. The agency notifies the interested party of requests for information.

       1. Prior to agency decision concerning release, supplier goes to federal district court seeking to review agency exercise of discretion, that is, court looks at the records and makes determination on applicability of exemptions.

       2. Some agencies have administrative procedures to consider supplier's arguments against disclosure; supplier exhausts administrative remedies, institutes suit upon final denial.

    B. Supplier hears of prospective disclosure.

III.   Comparing How Federal Agencies Approach the FOIA

    A. Federal Trade Commission (16 CFR 4.10)

       1. Lists confidential material exempted from disclosure—parallel to FOIA exemptions

       2. FTC's response to request.

         a. General Counsel determines all or part exempt.

         b. If exempt, requester petitions commission for disclosure—states purpose and interest in decision.

c. Commission exercises its discretion to release. Commission disclosure clearly based on intended use of information and requester's identification. Though contrary to legislative intent to disclose to "any person", regulations set standards for limiting disclosure to public, that is, may decide to give only to particular requester.

B. Food and Drug Administration (21 CFR 4)
1. Party considering submitting data requests determination whether all or part would be available to public.
2. Material held in confidence pending FDA determination.
3. Director of Bureau makes determination.
4. After decision, supplier can submit or withdraw his records. No copies kept if withdrawn.
5. If records determined *confidential* by FDA under exemption standards, then FDA will only make records available pursuant to court order [21 CFR 4.44(b)].

C. Department of Defense (40 FR 8190)
1. Requester advised of initial decision.
2. If request is for record received from nongovernmental source, source is notified where he is deemed to have protectable interest.
3. Source of information may comment before release or court determination.
4. A request denied may be appealed within military departments involved. Head of each component may reconsider a final decision to withhold if it involves matter of great public interest of DOD-wide consequence.

D. Environmental Protection Agency (40 CFR 2, and 40 FR 21987)
1. Initial determination regarding confidentiality of request for information.
2. Solicitation of comments of affected businesses.
3. Final determination.
4. Reasons to withhold data.
   a. Record exempt under 5 U.S.C. 552 (b).
   b. EPA decides as matter or discretion not to release; policy is to encourage disclosure unless third party shows prejudice to himself.

5. EPA guidelines for use of discretion
   a. Policy: won't apply discretion to certain exempt material including trade secrets and commercial or financial information obtained from a person and privileged or confidential [40 CFR 2.119(b)].
   b. Exceptions: Will release pursuant to federal court order; and exceptional circumstances under appropriate restrictions with approval of General Counsel.

Appendix 1B
Sample FOIA
Documents

UNITED STATES DISTRICT COURT
FOR THE DISTRICT OF COLUMBIA

(NAME OF REQUESTING PARTY)	)
	)
Plaintiff,	)
	)
v.	) Civil Action No.: _____
	)
(NAME OF AGENCY)	)
(address)	)
	)
Defendant.	)

COMPLAINT FOR DECLARATORY AND
INJUNCTIVE RELIEF

JURISDICTION

1. This is an action under the Freedom of Information Act (FOIA), 5 U.S.C. 552 (1976), to order the defendant(s) to produce for review and copying certain documents in its possession.

2. This Honorable Court has jurisdiction over this action pursuant to 5 U.S.C. 552(a)(4) and 28 U.S.C. 1331 (1976).

PARTIES

3. The plaintiff, (NAME), is (a description of the requesting party).

(continued)

Figure 1B–1. Sample FOIA Complaint

Figure 1B–1 continued

CAUSE OF ACTION

4. On (date of request), the plaintiff requested by letter (copy is attached hereto as Exhibit A) access under the FOIA to all records, reports, and memoranda pertaining to (description of what you are requesting) and in possession of the (name of agency).

5. On or about (date), the plaintiff's request was denied by the (name of agency) (copy of the demand letter is hereto attached as Exhibit B).

6. On or about (date), the plaintiff appealed said denial with (name head of agency) (copy of letter of appeal is hereto attached as Exhibit C); on or about (date), said appeal was denied (copy of letter of denial is hereto attached as Exhibit D).

7. The plaintiff has exhausted all administrative remedies, and pursuant to 5 U.S.C. 552(a) requests this Court to order the defendant(s) to allow plaintiff to review and copy the requested documents.

WHERETOFORE, the plaintiff prays that:

(a) the Court order the defendant(s) to produce the requested documents for review and copying;

(b) the Court grant the plaintiff attorney's fees and court costs; and

(c) any such other and further relief as the Court may deem just and proper.

_____
(NAME OF REQUESTING
PARTY OR COUNSEL)

Dated: City and State
       Date

UNITED STATES DISTRICT COURT
FOR THE DISTRICT OF COLUMBIA

(NAME OF REQUESTING PARTY)	))
Plaintiff,	))
v.	) Civil Action No.: _____)
(NAME OF GOVERNMENT AGENCY)	))
Defendant.	)

MOTION TO REQUIRE DETAILED
JUSTIFICATION, ITEMIZATION AND INDEXING

Now comes the plaintiff, (NAME), and moves this Court for an order requiring the defendant, (NAME OF AGENCY), to provide, within 30 days of the filing of the complaint in this action, a detailed itemization and index of the documents that have been withheld, including a description of the nature and contents of each document, and a detailed justification of the reasons supporting the claims that the requested documents are exempt from disclosure under the Freedom of Information Act, 5 U.S.C. 552 (1976). It is necessary that the defendant provide such a description and justification in order to enable the plaintiff to effectively argue and the court to knowledgeably decide whether the defendant's claims of exemption are proper. [See Vaughn v. Rosen, 484 F.2d 820, 826-28, cert. denied, 415 U.S. 977 (1974).]

Respectfully submitted,

_____

(NAME OF REQUESTING
PARTY OR HIS COUNSEL)

DATED: City and State
Date

Figure 1B–2. Sample FOIA Vaughn Motion

UNITED STATES DISTRICT COURT
FOR THE DISTRICT OF COLUMBIA

(NAME OF REQUESTING PARTY) (address) Plaintiff,	)))))
v.	) Civil Action No.: _____)
(NAME OF GOVERNMENT AGENCY) (address) Defendant.	)))))

ORDER

Upon consideration of the plaintiff's Motion To Require Detailed Justification, Itemization and Indexing, the memorandum of points and authorities in support thereof, the papers submitted by defendants in opposition thereto, and the full record herein, it is this _____day of _____, 19_____,

ORDERED, that the plaintiff's Motion To Require Detailed Justification, Itemization and Indexing be and is hereby granted, and it is further

ORDERED, that the defendant deliver, within 30 days of the filing of the Complaint in this action, to this Court and to counsel for the plaintiffs a detailed justification for its allegations that the requested documents are exempt from disclosure under the Freedom of Information Act, 5 U.S.C. 552, including an itemization and index which correlates specific statements in such justification with actual portions of the requested documents.

_____
United States District Judge

Figure 1B–3. FOIA Court Order

2 How to Safeguard Your Privacy

The General Accounting Office—Congress's watchdog agency—has warned that the Social Security Administration's (SSA) records on millions of U.S. citizens are not adequately safeguarded from potential abuse and misuse. For example, an employee of the SSA is alleged to have sold the names and addresses of several thousand recipients to a large life-insurance provider. In a separate case, an employee of the Internal Revenue Service (IRS) is said to have leaked confidential information on numerous taxpayers to credit-reporting bureaus. The federal government has yet to prosecute these individuals; unfortunately, invasions of privacy are not exceptional in Washington.

The public, however, does have legal recourse; it has available to it laws with which it can protect itself from corrupt and unethical bureaucrats. One of the more important of these laws is the Privacy Act (PA).[1] The act regulates both the collection and dissemination of personal information by the federal bureaucracy. It also authorizes an individual to request access to, and obtain copies of any files maintained on him by any of the federal executive agencies. He can do this directly or through an attorney.

The PA also allows an individual to contest the accuracy, pertinence, and timeliness of the records an agency maintains on him. The act requires that an agency, upon request by an individual, inform him of all the uses it has made of his personal records. However, it must deal only with regard to the individual's own records; the PA does not authorize the release, correction, or disclosure of records belonging to third parties.

Using the Privacy Act

If you should have cause to suspect that the Federal Bureau of Investigation (FBI) or any other federal agency has a file on you, contact its Privacy Act officer and request in writing that he provide you with copies of or access to your records. You may also request that your records be amended if you discover any inaccuracies.

However, as with the Freedom of Information Act (FOIA), be certain to identify the records involved as specifically as possible in regards to time, place, and location. Logic dictates that an agency's Privacy Act

23

office, inundated with thousands of requests annually, will pay scant attention to a general or vague request. A request that fails to identify the records in question will often be denied or go unanswered for long periods of time.

PA requests can be made either in person or by telephone, but writing is recommended because this serves to establish a chronological record. Should the agency fail to comply with your request, written documentation will be necessary if you resort to litigation. PA requests should be addressed to either the head of the agency or its Privacy Act officer. Both in your letter and on the envelope, be sure to specify that this is a Privacy Act request. (See figure 2–1 for a sample request.)

The act allows an individual to bring a lawsuit in federal court to

---

(Date) _____

TO: Privacy Officer
     (Name and address of agency)

RE: Privacy Act Request

Dear Sir:

Under the provisions of the Privacy Act of 1974 (5 U.S.C. 522a), I hereby request a copy of (describe as accurately and specifically as possible the records you want). If there are any fees for copying the records I am requesting, please inform me before you bill the request.

If all or any part of this request is denied, please cite the specific exemption(s) which you think justifies your refusal to release the information. Also, please inform me of your agency's appeal procedure.

                              Yours truly,
                              (Signature
                              Name
                              Address
                              Telephone)

Figure 2–1. Sample Privacy Act Request

enforce his right of access and also his right to request amendments to his personal records. If an agency should fail to comply with the PA, an individual can bring a lawsuit for damages if he can demonstrate that he was injured as a result of the refusal or failure to comply.

Scope and Objectives

Like the FOIA, the PA applies only to the executive branch of the federal government; it does not cover records collected or stored by many of the state or local agencies or private groups (although many states have similar privacy legislation). Unlike the FOIA, the act covers only data which is of a personal nature, and is collected, stored, and disseminated by the federal bureaucracy.

Under the PA, any person can place a request for access to his personal (not corporate) records. Unless these records fall within one or more of the act's exemptions (its general and specific exemptions will be discussed later in this chapter), the information cannot be withheld by the agency's staff.

Using the PA is simple and requires no legal skills. It was drafted with the layperson in mind; for example, a taxpayer who has been the target of an IRS investigation may request the agency's Privacy Act officer to allow him to review his files. In the majority of cases, however, PA requests have dealt with such things as access to one's military, medical, and arrest records, as well as an array of other personal and medical information compiled by the federal bureaucracy.

An individual placing a PA request need not explain why he wants access to or copies of his records, although an agency may and often does require verification of identity. This usually takes the form of requiring an individual to submit a copy of his birth certificate. Some agencies, however, will accept only requests with notarized signatures.

The act also provides for criminal sanctions against any person who knowingly and willfully requests or receives access to the personal records of a third party under false pretense. An individual who attempts to obtain or obtains such records and in the process uses the U.S. mails, faces prosecution under the federal mail-fraud statutes. Few of the federal agencies have referred such cases to the Department of Justice for criminal prosecution because the department has demonstrated little interest in such prosecutions.

As with the FOIA, the PA allows agencies to charge a nominal fee to cover photocopying costs, but few of the agencies charge such fees. The act also allows the agencies to charge fees for the time spent by their staffs in locating and preparing the requested records for inspection and copying. The PA provides a waiver of costs for indigents.

The Privacy Act imposes no time limitation on an agency to respond to a request. Federal guidelines do require, however, that agencies make some form of response within ten working days; in addition, these guidelines require that an agency, upon receipt of a request, inform the individual whether it will grant his request. If the agency consents to the request, it must inform the individual as to where and when he can review and copy the records.

The federal guidelines also require that an agency produce the requested records within a thirty-working-day period. As is the case with the FOIA, an agency can request an extension of time within which to respond to a PA request. Few of the agencies comply with the time schedules; long delays are the norm.

An individual can request that the records be turned over to his attorney; or that a nonlawyer (second party) be allowed to accompany and assist him in reviewing his records. In those cases where medical records are involved, an individual can request that these be turned over directly to his family physician for review. Some records are exempt from disclosure altogether; but the burden falls on the agency to justify its refusal.

General Exemptions

The Privacy Act outlines two categories of exempt material: general and specific. Records that fall within one of these exemptions need not be released by the agency. An individual has no right to review, copy, or amend records that are exempt under the act.

The act's general exemptions cover only the Central Intelligence Agency (CIA) and the federal criminal-investigatory agencies (for example, the FBI and the U.S. Secret Service). These general exemptions are often referred to as the *(J)(1)* and *(J)(2) exemptions*. The specific exemptions are known as the *K exemptions* [(K)(1) to (K)(7)].

The act's (J)(1) exemption covers only the CIA. It allows its director to exclude some of that agency's records from public disclosure. An individual can be denied access to his personal records by the CIA if these are (J)(1)-exempt material; in addition, an individual will not be allowed to correct, copy, or amend such records. However, an individual can sometimes gain access to his (J)(1)-exempt records by placing an FOIA request.

Records maintained by any of the federal criminal-investigatory agencies fall within the scope of the act's (J)(2) exemption. To qualify as (J)(2)-exempt material, an agency (or any of its subdivisions) must have as its principal function the enforcement of federal criminal laws. This includes all federal police efforts aimed at preventing, controlling, or reducing crime, as well as any efforts directed at apprehending criminals. The (J)(2) exemption also covers many of the records collected, stored, and disseminated by federal prosecutorial, correctional, and parole authorities.

The act's (J)(2) exemption specifically authorizes the heads of the criminal agencies to exclude many law-enforcement-related personnel records from disclosure. For example, the Director of the FBI can withhold any records that:

Are compiled solely for the purpose of identifying individual criminal offenders and alleged offenders;

Consist only of identifying data and notations of arrests, and the nature and disposition of a criminal case;

Consist only of information compiled for the purpose of a criminal investigation; or

Consist of reports of informants and/or investigators.

However, because bureaucrats often err, it is not unusual for an agency to unknowingly release exempt records.

When making a request for your personal file, it is sound strategy to employ both the FOIA and the PA. If an agency withholds the requested records on the grounds that they are exempt under the FOIA, it may nevertheless have to release them under the PA. For example, some criminal-investigatory files (once the investigation is completed) are open to review and inspection under the FOIA, though disclosure will be denied under a PA request. Thus, when you place a request for records, cite both statutes.

Specific Exemptions

The Privacy Act lists seven specific (K) exemptions. Unlike the general exemptions, these cover all of the federal agencies. The following records can be withheld by an agency under one or more of the specific exemptions.

Records that are classified as secret and deal with national-defense or foreign-policy interests.

Records of an investigatory nature that are gathered strictly for law-enforcement objectives.

The intelligence files of the U.S. Secret Service (specifically those that are maintained for the purpose of ensuring the safety of the President and other federal and foreign officials under Service protection).[2]

Records that are used solely for statistical purposes, including all IRS files of select individuals used by the agency to compute the national income averages.

All investigatory files used in making decisions concerning federal employment, contracts, and security clearances.

Any evaluation material used solely to make decisions regarding promotion of military personnel.

The primary objective of the specific exemptions is to safeguard the identity of confidential sources and informants; they also serve to ensure a modicum of privacy for some of the bureaucracy's inner workings. Thus, any efficiency report used by the military for purposes of making promotion decisions would be exempt. The act's drafters were of the opinion that to release such records would impact adversely on the military's promotion system and thus interfere with its efficiency and daily workings.

None of the act's exemptions (general or specific) can be employed by an agency to deny a legitimate FOIA request; nor can an FOIA exemption be used by an agency to deny a legitimate PA request. Thus, when requesting records that could possibly fall under one of the PA's exemptions, be sure to also cite the FOIA. Occasionally, an agency will release K-exempt records under an FOIA request. Regardless of whether an agency's records fall under one or more of the PA's exemptions, the agency continues to bear the responsibility for their accuracy, relevancy, and timeliness.

Handling Denials

Unlike the FOIA, the PA does not provide standard procedures for appealing an agency's denial of a request. However, many of the agencies have adopted their own internal procedures for handling PA appeals. These internal regulations often require that an agency's Privacy Act officer inform the requesting party of its procedures. If the officer should fail to do so, then you should request in writing that he inform or provide you with copies of the agency's appeal procedures (see figure 2–2). The agency should also (under its own internal rules) provide you with the name and address of its appeal officer. Not all of the agencies will provide you with that information, in which case you should write directly to the head of that agency. Your letter should be accompanied by copies of your original PA request and also the staff's denial.

A partial denial is handled procedurally as if it were a total refusal; the same applies for FOIA denials. In your PA appeal letter, be sure to address and rebut any and all of the staff's reasons for its refusal. In addition, detail the reasons why you should be granted access and attach copies of any documents that support your position. It is also good strat-

---

(Date) _____

TO: Privacy Officer
      (Name and address of agency)

RE: Privacy Act Appeal

Dear Sir:

By letter dated (give date) I requested that information held by your agency concerning me be amended. This request was denied, and I am hereby appealing that denial. For your information (detail relevant information as basis for your appeal.)

I trust that upon consideration of my reasons for seeking the desired changes, you will grant my request to amend the disputed material. However, in the event you refuse this request, please advise me of the agency procedures for filing a statement of disagreement.

Yours truly,
(Signature
Name
Address
Telephone)

Figure 2–2. Sample Letter to Appeal Privacy Act Denial

egy to cite the FOIA in your PA appeal; thus, if the agency denies your PA appeal, it may still feel compelled to grant part or all of your request on the basis of the FOIA.

Appeals are usually made within thirty working days from the date of receipt of the denial. An agency can, however, request a thirty-day extension to respond to your appeal. Even if the agency decides against an appeal, it must still allow you to submit a brief statement outlining your position. This statement is often referred to as a *disagreement statement*. The agency must incorporate it into your records; it becomes an integral part of your file, and must accompany it whenever a request is made for the file.

An agency's staff is allowed to submit its own statement rebutting the appellant's arguments. The staff's rebuttal statement is also incorporated in the appellant's file. The rebuttal statement summarizes the agency's position: why it refused to allow the appellant access to all or part of his records; and/or why it refused to allow him to amend those records.

Taking Your Case to Court

You can bring a PA-related lawsuit against an agency any time it refuses to allow you (or your attorney) access to your records; refuses to amend your records; denies your appeal; and/or fails to act upon either your initial request or appeal. Further, any person who has been adversely affected by an agency's failure or refusal to comply with the act may file a lawsuit for damages. For example, John Smith was denied a promotion at work because of erroneous information in his files with the FBI; if the FBI refuses to remedy these errors, Smith can sue (provided that the information at issue was collected by the FBI's staff).

Unlike the FOIA, the Privacy Act does not require an individual to exhaust all of the agency's internal administrative procedures before seeking relief in federal court; rather, he can file a lawsuit at any time. However, the act does require that an individual first exhaust an agency's internal appeal procedures when he is only contesting its refusal to amend his records.

Should the court find in favor of the plaintiff, it can direct the agency to allow him access to and/or an amendment of his records. In addition, the court can award the plaintiff monetary damages and court fees. The act also provides for the prosecution of any agency employee who knowingly and willfully fails to comply with its provisions; these criminal prosecutions are the province of the Department of Justice.

A plaintiff can file a lawsuit under the PA in any of the following jurisdictions: place of residence; place of business; locale in which the agency's records are located; or the District of Columbia. The act requires that all lawsuits be brought within two years from the date of the agency's refusal to comply with the plaintiff's request or appeal.

Agencies are required to maintain a detailed list of all disclosures they make or have made; the individual about whom these disclosures are made is entitled to review this list. Thus, when placing a PA request, be certain to also request access to or a copy of the disclosure list. Requests made by law-enforcement agencies, however, are exempt and will not appear on the list, nor will any disclosures made under FOIA requests.

The PA, when employed effectively, can assist the average citizen in safeguarding his privacy from bureaucratic encroachment. Unfortunately, in the bureaucratic jungle, only the knowledgeable survive.

Notes

1. See 5 U.S.C. 552(a).
2. See 18 U.S.C. 3056.

Appendix 2A
Analysis of the
Privacy Act

I. Objectives
   A. Protect individual privacy interests by regulation of federal agency practices concerning individuals.
      1. *Individual* is defined as a "citizen of U.S." -5 U.S.C. 552a(a)(2).
      2. Individual includes corporations in the sense that there is no separate legislation drafted to cover corporations.
   B. Give access to the individual about whom information is kept.
   C. Restrict acquisition, retention and dissemination of the information.
   D. The legislation deals primarily with personal information (such as welfare files and medical histories).

II. Disclosure Procedures
   A. Conditions [5 U.S.C. 552a(b)]
      1. Individual's records released only in response to written request by individual (subject) or written consent from subject to third party's request.
      2. Agency can disclose certain information.
         a. Disclosure required under FOIA
         b. To Bureau of Census
         c. National Archives
         d. Where health or safety affected
   B. Records must be kept of all disclosures except [5 U.S.C. 552a(c)].
      1. Information released to employees, including officials needing the records to carry out their duties
      2. Information released pursuant to FOIA
      3. Records given to agency for law-enforcement purposes
   C. Access by subject [5 U.S.C. 552a(d)]
      1. Examination
      2. Correction if inaccurate, irrelevant, or incomplete
      3. Agency refusal to correct
         a. Must notify individual of refusal
         b. Procedures for appeal
         c. Judicial review provision
   D. Agency requirements [5 U.S.C.A. 552a(e)]
      1. Collect what is "relevant and necessary" to accomplish purpose required by its organic act
      2. Acquire data from individual directly rather than from third source

3. Note in *Federal Register* systems of records in existence, location, use, and responsible official
4. Establish conduct rules for persons developing and operating records systems
5. Establish administrative, physical safeguards for protecting confidentiality
6. Publish proposed new uses of information in *Federal Register*

E. Agency Rules must be developed [5 U.S.C.A. 552a(f)] to respond to requests, identify individuals, provide review and appeal procedures.

F. Civil Remedies for individuals [5 U.S.C.A. 552a(g)(1)]
1. Individuals can sue in district court when agency fails to keep timely, correct records, or refuses to amend records.
2. Individual can get injunction against improper withholding of records from him.
3. Individual can seek damages where agency intentionally fails to keep accurate records or to otherwise comply with rules.

G. Criminal Penalties: Officials with access to records individually identifiable, who willfully disclose material they know is protected by the act, are subject to misdemeanor penalties.

H. General Exemptions [5 U.S.C.A. 522a(j)]: No right to notice, access or challenge
1. Records for law enforcement
2. CIA records

I. Specific Exemptions [5 U.S.C.A. 552a(k)]: No right to notice, access, or challenge
1. Classified documents
2. Secret Service files
3. Federal employment examination and testing records
4. Where informant identity revealed; for example, to determine suitability for military service or government contracts.
5. Records solely for statistical purposes; for example, Census Bureau.

J. Government Contractors [5 U.S.C. 552a(m)
1. Requirements of act apply to systems operated by or on behalf of agency by contract to accomplish an agency function
2. Contractor and employees considered agency employed for purposes of criminal penalties

Appendix 2B
Key Privacy Federal
Statutes and
Regulations

A. Statutes
   1. Privacy Act (5 U.S.C. 552a)
   2. Trade Secrets Act (18 U.S.C. 1905)
   3. Fair Credit Reporting Act (15 U.S.C. 1681)
   4. Buckley Amendments to Educational Act (12 U.S.C. 1232)
   5. Right to Financial Privacy Act (12 U.S.C. 3401–3422)
B. Regulations
   1. OMB Circular A–108 (July 1, 1975)—Delineates federal agency responsibility pursuant to the Privacy Act.
   2. 41 CFR 101–35.17—Outlines user and provider agency responsibilities when there is intercourse between two agencies touching upon Privacy Act records.
   3. 41 CFR 1–1.327 (Federal Requirement Regulations)—Seeks to enhance the Privacy of Individuals.
   4. 5 CFR 1–293 (A)—Details regulations as to personnel record systems within federal agencies.
   5. 28 CFR 20.30–20.38 (Federal System and Interstate Exchange of Criminal History Record Information)—All federal agencies must sign compliance. Regulations pertaining to disseminations of information by agencies having direct access to the FBI's computerized National Crime Information Center.
C. Guidelines
   1. 40 FR 28949—OMB Guidelines interpretive of the Privacy Act.
   2. 44 FR 23138—Supplementary OMB Guidelines for Implementation of the Privacy Act of 1974: Matching Programs Conducted by Federal Agencies.

35

3 Getting Your Way with Congress

Increasingly, the U.S. Congress has come to dominate our daily lives through a multiplicity of legislation. The legislative process itself has become so complex and fraught with loopholes that we have come to rely on lobbyists and consultants to lead us through this maze. Anticipating congressional events and staying ahead of the process requires not only a grasp of its jargon, but also a knowledge of the workings of its members and committees.

Understanding this process and knowing how to utilize an array of congressional resources (readily available to the public at large) will enable the public to better gain the ears of Congress. It is ignorance, rather than malfeasance, which often keeps the citizenry out of the federal legislative process.

How Congress Operates

The power of Congress varies and often depends on who is in the White House. The public often mistakenly connects Congress only with the power to legislate. Congress and its committees, however, are also responsible for: carrying out investigations of the executive branch; monitoring the federal bureaucracy; approving treaties; raising and lowering taxes; approving bureaucratic and judicial appointments; and appropriating funds. Although the President can veto congressional legislation, a two-thirds majority vote in each chamber can override his veto. In addition, Congress polices itself. Only Congress (each chamber) passes on the qualifications of its members. (For information about Congressional members see appendix 3A.)

The work of preparing and scrutinizing legislation is handled largely by the committees of each chamber. There are fifteen standing committees in the Senate and twenty-two in the House of Representatives. Each committee in turn is composed of several subcommittees; there are also joint committees composed of members from both chambers. Whenever necessary, each chamber has the power to establish special investigative committees to look into matters of concern to the Congress. Members of standing committees are selected in each chamber by the vote of their peers. The membership of the special committees and subcommittees is selected by established rules and procedures.

If you have any questions about the Congress, address these as follows: questions on the Senate to the Secretary's Office, Room S–221, Capitol Building; and questions on the House to the House, Room H–105, Capitol Building. The following information and resources are readily available from Congress on written request:

substantive legislation under consideration;

amendments;

action on legislation;

conference committee reports;

treaties received or reported;

major nominations received, confirmed, or withdrawn;

legislative reports;

nonlegislative reports;

all substantive speeches by members of Congress;

committee schedules;

committee membership list; and

public laws.

How Legislation Moves

Bills are introduced by members of Congress in their respective chambers. Once a bill is introduced, it automatically goes to the appropriate committee. The chairperson of that committee will refer it to a subcommittee for review. Unless it is successfully acted upon by the subcommittee, the bill never goes before the full committee. In a subcommittee the bill's supporters, opponents, and other interested parties can offer written or verbal testimony. If a bill affects a specific federal agency, the congressional liaison staff of that agency may also offer testimony in support of or opposition to the bill. Amendments to the bill can be introduced when it is before a subcommittee or committee, or at the time it is on the floor of the chamber.

If the subcommittee acts favorably on the bill, it is then forwarded to the full committee for action. In the committee the legislation will again come under scrutiny; it will be supported or opposed by numerous groups with an interest in the outcome. If the bill is approved by a majority of the members of the committee, it is then sent to the floor of its chamber (with recommendations) for debate and a vote.

If a bill passes, it is then sent to the other chamber for action. The second chamber will refer it to an appropriate committee. Before it leaves this committee and goes to the floor for debate, it must be approved by a majority of the committee members. If approved on the floor of the second chamber, conferees from both chambers are selected to work out the necessary compromises between the two separate versions of the bill. The conferees will then prepare a conference report. Once the report is approved by both chambers, the legislation is forwarded to the President for signing. If it is signed, it will become law; if the President should refuse to sign it and sends the bill back to the chamber where it originated with his written objections, this constitutes a veto. Both chambers can override his veto by a two-thirds vote.

However, if a bill is not acted upon in the session in which it is introduced, it will die with that two-year session. It must then be reintroduced in the next session if it is to be reconsidered. More than 20,000 bills are introduced in each session of Congress. Fewer than 10 percent of these are reported out of committee; of those that are, fewer than 5 percent become law. For a congressional bill to be enacted into law, it must either have a powerful constituency and/or little opposition.

Dealing with Committee Chairpersons

A committee chairperson is a powerful figure in Congress. Members of the public contact a chairperson for various reasons. Most often, they will do so to:

express support or opposition to a bill, program, or nomination; or to express an interest to appear and offer testimony before the committee;

seek to influence the rules, policies, or internal decisions of a federal department or agency;

express views regarding policies and programs of the executive office;

seek to initiate or defeat legislation;

affect funds appropriated to a program or agency.

However, even a powerful committee chairperson can do little to help you if a bill has already reached the floor of the chamber. Once a bill has reached the floor, you should turn your efforts to the appropriate committee in the other chamber; but the second chamber will take no action until the first chamber has acted.

Committee chairpersons exert powerful influence over the path of legislation. They can assign the bill to a subcommittee for hearings and review, or they can keep it in the full committee to exert maximum control over its future. However, committee chairpersons are responsive to pressure from powerful constituencies; a chairperson's power has limits.

In order to increase your effectiveness, try to coordinate your lobbying efforts with those of other groups. Your arguments for or against the legislation should be presented in terms of issues that strike the ear of the chairperson's constituents. As a general rule, committee chairpersons are more susceptible and sensitive to pressures that emanate from constituencies in their districts or states, rather than those of corporations and groups based in other states. Their power base rests on what their electorate feels and thinks.

In some instances a powerful chairperson (especially one who has ambitions for national office) may take special interest in various national issues. If your interests coincide, you may find that his staff will prove receptive to some form of cooperative effort. The underlying rule when dealing with a chairperson is to first identify his needs and constituency, and then to demonstrate how, by supporting your interests, he is at the same time advancing his own. If he does not agree, continue to be polite as you may plan to call on him for assistance in the future.

How to Seek the Support of Members

If you should have to solicit the support of members of Congress, there are three guidelines to remember: be polite; be well prepared; and be persistent. Know your facts well and present them in understandable language; also ensure that your data is accurate. Whenever preparing for a meeting with a member of Congress or his staff, be sure to:

Review the member's voting record. This will help you to better assess his potential views on the bill which concerns you.

Check with consumer, business, and other groups that deal with and/or rate members of Congress. Draw on their experience.

You must contact the member's appointment secretary or office manager to request a meeting. Briefly inform the secretary or office manager of the purpose of your meeting and of other people who will be present. Give their names, titles, and the purpose for their attendance.

Once a meeting has been set up, your group should agree in advance who will be the spokesperson. Also carefully review and (if need be) rehearse your presentation. You should be prepared to address the flaws of your position and also those of your opponent's position. During the meeting, present the facts in a concise and orderly manner. Make sure that your statements are accurate and factual; erroneous or false statements and data can seriously undermine your credibility and position.

In the meeting, discuss the potential impact of the legislation on your constituency or industry. Also remind the member of the impact on his state or district; be prepared to detail its impact on industries and/or groups of import to the member. You will want to point out the positive and negative aspects of the legislation, and how these will affect his political career. Whenever possible, have someone from his district or state accompany you to the meeting.

Before the meeting is ended you should:

Leave a brief written statement (which summarizes your position) with the member or his staff;

Answer all questions raised by the member or his staff in a factual, polite, and professional manner;

Request that the member at least give consideration to your position;

Thank both the member and his staff (and follow this up with a letter).

Although a personal meeting with a member of Congress is desirable and recommended, this may not always be possible. If you cannot arrange for a meeting, forward a written statement of your position to him. In preparing your letter, consider the following guidelines.

Confine yourself to one area or subject.

Limit your letter to two or three pages (250 words per page) and summarize your position in the first page.

Avoid extreme philosophical and ideological positions, and address yourself to the member's basic need of reelection.

Be specific as to the bill or program (list number and/or title) you are writing about.

Detail some of your efforts to date.

Include not only your name, title, and address, but also make reference to other groups with which you are affiliated and who share your basic views (especially if some of these are from the member's state or district).

Always address members of the House as Mr., Ms, or Mrs., and Senators as Sen.

Keep in mind that members of Congress have busy schedules. They are often too busy to be well informed on an issue. It is your job to both educate and convince them of the merits of your position.

Handling the Staff

Many of the decisions on legislation and policy are made not by a congressional member, but rather by his staff. It is important to clearly identify who the key staffers are, and get to know them both professionally and socially. Make it a practice to maintain periodic contacts with them; if you are in Washington, visit their offices.

The key staff person in a senator's office is his Administrative Assistant (AA). He is often the staffer with the closest ties to the senator; he sees his boss often on a daily basis. His attitudes, politics, biases, and political perceptions will often reflect and influence those of his boss. Because your initial contacts with a senator's office may leave a lasting impression on the AA, make sure that these will be positive.

Another important Senate staffer is the senator's Legislative Assistant (LA). The LA is often a lawyer by training and may also have some government experience. It is the LA's job to keep the senator abreast of legislation within his committees and legislation that may be of interest to the senator's constituents. It is also his job to ensure that the senator will not alienate powerful pressure groups.

The senator's Personal Secretary (PS) can also be an important member of the staff. The PS controls access to the senator; all appointments must first be cleared by the secretary. It is the PS who screens undesirables and brings some order to the senator's daily life.

A smaller but parallel structure is found in the office of the House member. However, because House members have smaller staffs, the AA will often also act as the LA. When dealing with a House member, address your initial contacts to his AA, who will be important to your later dealings with the House member.

Another important staffer is the House member's Office Manager (OM). The OM handles the member's appointment calendar, and keeps him abreast of any important office developments. The OM acts as a personal secretary.

In addition, members of Congress (both House and Senate) maintain offices and staffs in their respective home districts or states. These staffs may be of value to you when dealing with the member. Get to know them; understand their political needs, and do not hesitate to approach them with your requests.

Communicating with the Committees

Since the congressional committees (and their subcommittees) are the repositories of all legislation, it is important that you understand how they operate and how best to influence their decision making. The committees, however, are also arenas where competing interests battle daily. It is in the committees and subcommittees where legislation either survives or dies; where your opponents will marshal their forces and lay their traps. Remember that important decisions at the committee and subcommittee level are made by its chairperson, chief counsel, staff director, and its most senior member. The path of a bill, and its ultimate success, will largely depend on these key persons.

Senior members, because of their length of service and the political contacts they have made, are often well versed in the committee's operations. They are in tune with the everyday realities of Congress; they know where power lies and how to get a bill through a committee. In addition, congressional etiquette requires that they be accorded at least a semblance of deference by the junior members of the committee. The strong support of a senior member can help you prevail; at the minimum, it will ensure that other committee members will listen.

Testifying before a committee may advance your case. If you want to testify, contact the committee's chief counsel and request that you be allowed to do so. Telephonic requests should always be followed by a written confirmation. Specify why you are interested in the legislation, and also the group(s) you represent. List also the date and time (morning or afternoon) you would prefer to give testimony.

If the committee counsel appears reluctant to comply with your request, contact either the office of the committee chairperson or that of a senior member to inform them of your interest in testifying. If you are told it is not possible to offer verbal testimony because of scheduling problems, then request that you be allowed to submit a written statement and that this statement be incorporated in the committee's record. These statements should be mailed to the committee's director with a written request that they be distributed to committee members and incorporated in the committee's written report. (Check with the staff as to the number of copies of your submission they need; since there may be several reports, send a submission for each.)

If you are invited to give oral testimony, you have the right to be accompanied to the hearing by counsel of your choice. Before the hearing you will probably be contacted by the staff of those committee members who are favorably disposed to your position. They will want to review your testimony and may also request that you assist them in preparing questions that will be asked of you at the hearing. They may also ask for suggestions on questions to be put to other witnesses. Oral testimony, however, will sway few committee votes. But if delivered and orchestrated well, it can serve to present your position and possibly attract press coverage.

Committee hearings have been compared to a Broadway show; drama and theatrics are important ingredients. They serve to catch the attention of the news media, especially of the television evening news. Thus, be sure to provide the news media in advance with copies of your testimony; also ask the staff (those who are favorably disposed) to invite their press sources to the hearings.

If possible, have a member of Congress accompany you to the hearing. He need not be a member of the committee holding the hearing. If he accompanies you, his presence will prove of assistance since members of Congress are usually afforded courtesy by the other members and their staffs.

If a member should agree to testify on behalf of your position, this too will serve you well since his testimony will carry greater weight than yours with the committee. When preparing your presentation, keep it brief, get to your point and stick to it. Also, be prepared to address opposing views.

Your testimony should point out the strengths of your position. Be factual and if possible employ charts and exhibits, especially if these will have a dramatic effect. Carefully review your testimony prior to the hearing and anticipate cross-examination by hostile committee members or staffers. Coordinate your testimony with groups that have similar interests. Your allies may prove to be government officials.

Remember that a committee hearing is a stage that affords you the opportunity to transmit and air your views in public. The news media is an integral part of this process; it can help or undermine your case. Anticipate hostile questions—remember that your opponents are using this same forum to advance their views.

Influencing the Agencies

Congress has delegated some of its legislative powers to a growing body of regulatory agencies, such as the Interstate Commerce Commission

(ICC) and the Federal Trade Commission (FTC). These agencies have traditionally been responsive to the Congress; they are its creatures. Congress has guarded its jurisdiction over them zealously. Agency heads are subject to senatorial confirmation and many of their top officials come from congressional staffs. These agencies constitute a part of the Washington old-boy network.

Congress is also the source of authorizing legislation for these regulatory agencies. It not only appropriates funds for them, but also specifies how these funds are to be used. Congressional committees (and their chairpersons) exert powerful influence over these agencies; thus, the public can have an impact on an agency's decision making through the congressional route. By contacting the appropriate committee, you can exert indirect influence over the federal bureaucrats.

However, the agencies have powerful friends in Congress; they also have the support of important business groups who stand to gain from their regulations. These groups often have powerful resources to draw upon; they understand how Congress does business. If you plan to battle with one of the agencies, you should prepare your offensive well. Join forces with other groups and also other government agencies; for example, the Antitrust Division of the U.S. Department of Justice is not a friend of the Federal Trade Commission. Be sure to coordinate your efforts with friendly committee members and staffs. Your campaign should be subtle, but well prepared for any contingency that may arise. Since many committees are understaffed and lacking in the resources needed to adequately scrutinize the regulatory agencies, be ready to assist friendly committee staffs with studies, facts, evidence, and expert witnesses.

If you should threaten an agency's survival, be prepared to lock horns with it for a long time to come. The bureaucracy has learned to survive all adversities; administrations have come and gone, but the agencies continue. However, if you are tenacious the agency may be open to accommodation.

Congressional Sources of Information

Congress is both a source of legislation and information. Its many committees and offices churn out a multitude of studies and reports. It investigates and oversees every aspect of our social, economic, and political fiber; few industries or agencies escape its gaze. This valuable information is readily available, often for free, to the public at large. It is merely a question of knowing where to look.

Information on legislation, for example, is often available at no cost from the House Status Office. This office can supply you with the following.

The names and numbers of any bills.

An update on any given bill or committee hearing.

The sponsor of a bill and the date it was introduced, as well as the committee or subcommittee with jurisdiction over the legislation.

The committee or subcommittee that plans to hold hearings on a given bill and when those hearings will be held.

A list of related legislation, and contact with the appropriate committee, subcommittee, or member's office.

Once you have contacted the appropriate committee or subcommittee on some specific legislation, you should request:

A copy of the bill and any of its amendments.

Copies of reports, testimony, or hearings on the legislation.

The status of the bill and analogous legislation, and the committee's schedule for planned hearings.

The prospect that the bill will be voted out of committee.

Copies of bills, reports, and legislation enacted into law can easily be obtained by writing to the Document Room of the appropriate chamber. When writing you should list the number of the bill, indicate the number of copies you want sent to you, and enclose a self-addressed, self-adhesive label. As a matter of practice, limit your requests to no more than five bills in one request.

For additional information on legislation, you should review the *Congressional Record* and the *Information Service Index*. For a legislative update, you can contact the Senate or House Cloak Rooms, which play recorded update messages. You can also contact the Senate or House libraries for information; their telephone numbers are readily available by contacting the Capitol Hill Switchboard.

Another important congressional source is the General Accounting Office (GAO).[1] It is empowered to assist the Congress, its committees, and members in carrying out their legislative and oversight responsibilities. This office assists congressional committees and members in conducting investigations and in drafting proposed legislation.

The GAO has extensive audit authority which extends to all departments and agencies of the federal apparatus. Its staff has the power to examine, copy, and analyze any books, documents, papers, and records of any federal department or agency. The GAO may also investigate any matter that deals with the receipt, disbursement, and application of federal funds. In addition, its audit powers extend to both wholly and partially owned government corporations, and to contracts the federal government has with state and local governments, and private groups.

The Office of Technology Assessment (OTA) is another important source.[2] Its purpose is to assist the Congress in studying, planning, and reviewing the uses and impact of technology. The OTA assists congressional committees with studies that deal with a broad range of technology-related issues. The agency is authorized to obtain (from any federal department or agency) information, suggestions, statistics, and other necessary assistance for the purpose of carrying out its delegated functions. (For further sources of congressional information see appendix 3B.)

Congress and its bureaucracy constitute a powerful force in the federal governmental structure. Since the end of World War II it has become an active partner in the running of our national government. It has continued to remain politically responsive to public opinion. An understanding of how Congress operates is a must for anyone who wants to influence the outcome of federal legislation.

Notes

1. See, 31 U.S.C. 41.
2. See, 86 Stat. 797.

Appendix 3A
Rating Members of
Congress

A number of Washington-based organizations rate members of Congress. Each group selects a list of votes a congressman has cast and rates his performance according to their interests and ideologies. These lists and the organization's ratings are often available upon request:

Americans for Constitutional Action
955 L'Enfant Plaza, S.W.
Washington, D.C. 20024

Americans for Democratic Action
1424 16th Street, N.W.
Washington, D.C. 20036

Common Cause
2030 M Street, N.W.
Washington, D.C. 20036

Committee on Political Action
AFL–CIP
815 16th Street, N.W.
Washington, D.C. 20006

National Association of Businessmen
1000 Connecticut Avenue, N.W.
Washington, D.C. 20036

Taxation with Representation
Suite 210, 732 17th Street, N.W.
Washington, D.C. 20006

League of Women Voters
1730 M Street, N.W.
Washington, D.C. 20036

Ripon Society
1609 Connecticut Avenue, N.W.
Washington, D.C. 20009

National Farmers Union
1012 14th Street
Washington, D.C. 20005

American Conservative Union
316 Pennsylvania Avenue, S.E.
Washington, D.C., 20003

Consumer Federation of America
1012 14th Street, N.W.
Washington, D.C. 20005

American Security Council
1101 17th Street, N.W.
Washington, D.C. 20036

Appendix 3B
Tapping Congressional
Resources

Congress is a labyrinth; however, within it are found invaluable sources of information on its workings and those of the federal government. Learn your way around it by tapping the following sources. (Telephone numbers for offices in the Capital, House, and Senate can be obtained from the Capitol Switchboard.)

General Sources

Source	*Information*
Bill Status Office	Legislative status for both House and Senate bills
Congressional Record Index Clerk	Legislative history
Executive Clerks Office	Information on whether a bill has become law or been vetoed
General Accounting Office, Reports Department	Availability and ordering of GAO reports
Office of Federal Register, Statutes Branch	Public law numbers, statutory references
Federal Register	Highlights of items to be published in next day's issue
Government Printing Office	Order desk for general materials, including back issues of Congressional Record
Phototduplication Service, Library of Congress	Information on duplicating materials unavailable from document rooms and committees
Library of Congress	Telephone Inquiry Public Reference Section

Source	*Information*
Senate Majority Leader	Scheduling information, procedure
Senate Minority Leader	Scheduling information, procedure
Secretary of the Senate	Calendars, membership rosters, committee and subcommittee lists
Senate Democratic Cloakroom	Scheduling information, floor action
Senate Republican Cloakroom	Scheduling information, floor action
Democratic Policy Committee	Scheduling information
Republican Policy Committee	Scheduling information
Senate Parliamentarian	Procedural matters
Executive Clerk	Treaties and nominations
Enrolling Clerk	Whether bill has been signed and sent to White House
Senate Librarian	Legislative reference, current legislative status
Daily Digest	Questions re *Congressional Record,* Senate section "Summary at Back"
Office of Legislative Counsel	Draft legislation for senators, committees

House Sources

Source	*Information*
House Majority Leader	Scheduling information, procedure
House Minority Leader	Republication positions
Office of the Speaker	Information on scheduling, procedure

Democratic Cloakroom	Scheduling information, floor action
Republican Cloakroom	Scheduling information, floor action
Democratic Caucus	Scheduling information, positions, legislative prospects
House Parliamentarian	Procedural matters
Daily Digest	Information on the results of House committee meetings and floor action
Clerk of the House	Membership rosters, committee and subcommittee membership lists
Bill Clerk	Locating status of a bill (when other sources fail)
Enrolling Clerk	Whether bill has been signed and sent to the White House
Office of Legislative Counsel	Draft legislation for Congressmen, committees
Office of Law Revision Counsel	U.S. Code Revision enactment of codes into positive law
House Librarian	Legislative history
Democratic Steering and Policy Committee	Committee assignments, party legislative program
Democratic Study Group	Scheduling information
Republican Policy Committee	Scheduling information
Republican Research Committee	Background on legislation

Appendix 3C
Laws from which
Congress Is Exempt

Congress has taken care to ensure that an array of important federal laws do not apply to it. Among these are the:

Freedom of Information Act which provides for the disclosure of federal government information.

Privacy Act which regulates the disclosure of confidential personnel-related information.

Age Discrimination in Employment Act which makes it illegal to discriminate in employment on the basis of age.

Equal Pay Act which makes it illegal to discriminate on the basis of sex when setting wages.

Civil Rights Act which makes it illegal to discriminate on the basis of race, color, sex, age, or national origin.

Occupational Safety and Health Act which prescribes standards for the workplace.

4 Avoiding Expensive Washington Talent

The Freedom of Information and Privacy Acts are only two (albeit important) of the many tools that can assist you when dealing with the federal government. Learning how to employ these tools will enable you to have an input in the workings of the federal government; for example, you will be able to attend important agency hearings and obtain transcripts of their closed meetings, complete with the names of those in attendance.

By understanding how and when to use important federal laws and regulations, you will open up the decision-making process of the bureaucracy, and also have an input in their rule-making process. Much of this can be done without the need for expensive lawyers, lobbyists, and consultants. All you need is a grasp of these basic tools, the willingness to apply them, and some self-confidence.

How Government in the Sunshine Works

The Sunshine Act (SA) provides that it should be government policy to allow the public access to the fullest possible information concerning the decision-making process of the federal government.[1] Among other things, the SA requires that all agencies headed by two or more individuals open their meetings to the public at large. The act covers the independent regulatory agencies, advisory committees, U.S. Postal Service, and (with the exception of the cabinet departments) all other executive-branch agencies.

Further, the act requires federal agencies to make public announcements of the time, place, and subject matter of their meetings; they are required to disclose whether the meetings will be open or closed to the public. An agency must list the name and telephone number of the official designated to answer questions about its meetings; and the minutes or a transcript of the meetings must be made available to the public upon request. Many agencies have issued their own rules of compliance with the act, which can be obtained by contacting a specific agency directly.

The act defines an agency's meetings as any deliberation of at least the number of individuals required to take action by that agency. Meetings can only be closed at the request of any individual affected by the agency's deliberations, or by a vote of the majority of those persons required to take action. However, if the latter is the case, any member of the public can request the agency to provide him, within one day of the vote, with a written explanation of why its meeting will be closed.

Further, you can also request the agency to provide you with a list of all those persons that will be present at the closed meeting. If the agency fails to comply with your request, you can bring a lawsuit in a U.S. district court to enforce these provisions of the act; the agency then must justify its position. The act also provides for the award of attorneys fees and court costs should you prevail. However, if your action is without merit, the agency can request that the court order you to pay all court costs.

The SA also requires agencies, on an annual basis, to report to the Congress the number of meetings they have had and the reasons why some of them were closed. The act prohibits ex parte communications between agency officials and individuals with an interest in its pending business. In addition, agencies are required to publish notices of all their meetings (open or closed) in the *Federal Register*.

However, an agency can choose to close its meetings any time:

1. It deals with matters related to national defense or foreign policy;
2. The information to be discussed is classified by executive order;
3. The hearing will deal only with agency personnel rules and practices;
4. It is required by statute that the material to be discussed be kept confidential;
5. Trade secrets and other financial or commercial confidential data will be covered;
6. The matters to be discussed if made public would constitute an invasion of privacy;
7. The meeting will deal with investigatory matters related to law enforcement;
8. The meeting will deal only with bank examination records and related financial audits;
9. The information to be discussed if made public would endanger the financial stability of financial institutions;
10. The hearing will deal with the agency's involvement in legal proceedings; or
11. The information to be discussed deals exclusively with accusations of a crime.

Using the Administrative Procedure Act

The Administrative Procedure Act (APA) requires that federal agencies hold hearings on all of their proposed rules and that they provide the public with notice.[2] These notices must be published in the *Federal Register* and must include: a statement of the time, place, and nature of the public rule-making proceeding; reference to the authority under which the rule is proposed; and the terms of the proposed rule.

An individual or corporation wishing to participate in the rule-making process need only inform the agency (in writing) of its intension. An interested party can either testify in person before the agency or offer written comments on the proposed rule(s). However, if an agency fails to either provide notice of its proposed rule making, or to accord members of the public an opportunity to comment on it, then any aggrieved party can bring a lawsuit in a federal court to enforce the act's provisions.

Access to the rule-making process of any agency is a source of valuable information and also ensures that you have an input in rules that may affect you; the APA provides you with that opportunity. It is an important and valuable tool that, when properly used, can enhance public participation in the governing process.

Value of the *Federal Register*

Published daily, the *Federal Register (FR)* serves to update federal regulations. Federal documents appearing in the *FR* can be found under one of the following five headings: Presidential Documents; Rules and Regulations; Proposed Rules; Notices; and Sunshine Meetings. Federal agencies are required by law to publish all their rules and regulations in the *FR* at least thirty days before they take effect.

Announcements of Advisory Committee meetings are also required by law to be published in the *FR*, as are all notices of agency hearings, investigations, decisions, and rulings. All filings of petitions and applications before a federal agency are also required to be published in the *FR*.

All proposed agency modifications or changes in regulations also appear in the *FR*. Each proposed rule-making change carries with it an invitation for members of the public to participate in the process; this can be done by submitting either a written or verbal statement.[3]

Many of the federal regulations that are of concern to the public are found in the *FR;* by learning how to use it, you will be able to keep abreast of important developments in the federal government. The Office of the Federal Register (OFR) conducts periodic educational workshops on how to best use the *Federal Register;* these are open to members of the public at no cost. For information on these workshops, contact the OFR in Washington, D.C.

The federal government publishes an array of valuable publications for researchers, consultants, and other professionals. Many of the following can be purchased for a small fee by writing to the Superintendent of Documents, U.S. Government Printing Office, Washington, D.C. 20402.

Annual U.S. Government Manual

Annual Congressional Directory

Congressional Record

Commerce Business Daily

U.S. Government Purchasing and Sales Directory

Directory of Companies Required to File Annual Reports with the Securities and Exchange Commission

Federal Advisory Committees Index

U.S. Industrial Outlook

Economic Report of the President

Code of Federal Regulations and Other Sources

The *Code of Federal Regulations (CFR)* is an annual compilation of the regulations of all the federal agencies. It is revised at least once each year and is broken down into fifty broad subject areas. Each federal agency is assigned a chapter within the *CFR*, and the agencies are listed alphabetically. The *CFR* can serve as a convenient reference for enacted federal regulations; it also offers an in-depth summary of the powers, jurisdiction, and role of each of the executive agencies. For a review and discussion of each of the federal agencies and their enacted rules, you would do well to turn to the *CFR*.

A multitude of other federal government publications are also readily available to members of the public. The more important of these include:

Presidential Documents. These are weekly compilations of presidential announcements, transcripts of news conferences, messages to Congress, public speeches and remarks, and other material released by the White House.

Public Papers of the President. These are a companion to the *Presidential Documents,* providing a summary of materials released by the White House for each year. They also list presidential appointments and nominations.

Slip Laws. These are pamphlets of each public and private bill enacted by Congress and are issued several days after the statute becomes law.

Catalogue of United States Publications. Published monthly, it lists all publications issued by the federal departments and agencies for the previous month. It is available from the Superintendent of Documents, Government Printing Office, Washington, D.C. 20402.

Federal Information Centers are maintained by the General Service's Administration (GSA) in a number of major cities across the country. The centers provide the public with information on various areas dealing with the federal government. The information you want may be readily available by visiting, telephoning, or writing to the area center. A list of their locations is available by writing to the GSA, Washington, D.C.

There are also Federal Depository Libraries located across the country. These are the repositories of many important governmental publications including the *Federal Register* and *Code of Federal Regulations*.

The federal government has been called an open book. The following information sources are often available simply for the asking.

United States Statutes at Large: contain all federal statutes, joint and concurrent resolutions of Congress, presidential proclamations, reorganization plans, and constitutional amendments.

United States Reports: contain all decisions and orders of the Supreme Court. In it are found the full texts of all signed opinions, a record of orders granting or denying a petition for a writ of certiorari, per curiam decisions, rulings of the Court on its obligation to accept appeals cases for review, and opinions of individual justices in chambers.

United States Supreme Court Records and Briefs: contain all briefs and other officially docketed materials relating to cases brought before the Court.

Index to Code of Federal Regulations: provides comprehensive access to the *CFR*. It is published annually, and includes cross-referenced subject and geographic indexes, plus supplementary lists of descriptive and reserved *CFR* headings.

Congressional Record (CR): is the official transcript of debates and other floor proceedings of the U.S. Congress. In it are also found documents and speeches placed on the record by members of Congress, and the texts of bills, presidential messages, treaties, and various other materials important to legislative and political research. There are two versions of the *CR:* a daily paper edition; and an annual edition. The *CR* is available from the Superintendent of Documents, Washington, D.C.

Many individuals and businesses mistakenly retain the services of expensive Washington experts to do for them what they can easily do for themselves. Much of the information is already public and it is only a question of knowing where to find it. The federal government itself and many of its publications can prove to be valuable sources of information.

Notes

1. See, P.L. 94–409. The text of the act appears in the U.S. Code, Title V, chapter 5, subchapter II, section 552b.

2. See, Title V, chapter 5, subchapter 2 and Title V, chapter 7 of the U.S.C.

3. The Administrative Procedure Act also makes reference to this requirement.

5 Understanding the Press

With a population of more than two thousand correspondents, Washington, D.C., can easily boast that it has the largest contingent of journalists in the world. Thus, whether you want to call on the press corps for assistance or to rebut an opponent's position, it behooves you to understand the behavior and informal rules of conduct of the press. This cadre of men and women have their own mores and ethics.

The Washington press corps ranges from the ethical to the disreputable; from the highly qualified to the mediocre. Some do their own research, while others rely on the press releases of private and public groups. They have a job to do, and would like to do it by exerting as little time and effort as possible.

Rules of the Game

Whenever you deal with a member of the press corps, remember that there are certain fundamental rules that govern the journalist's behavior. Make it your job to both understand them and comply with them; trying to change the rules can prove costly. What you say and how you say it is extremely important in the press game; members of the press do not like to be fooled. You need not tell them everything, but be certain that what you tell them is accurate.

Members of the press stake their credentials and reputations on statements that they attribute to their sources. If the statements turn out to be false, a journalist's standing with his peers may suffer; his professional reputation may be tarnished forever. A journalist stakes his credibility and career on the information that you supply him; should you mislead him, it may only serve to haunt you in the long run.

The journalist can let the word out in his circles that you are not to be trusted; in turn, your own credibility and professional reputation may suffer. In a town where the press is an active player, this may hurt you and undermine your efforts. Thus, either play it straight, or simply tell them that you are not prepared to play; even the most persistent of the press corps will usually understand.

When dealing with members of the press, remember that they are generalists. Avoid technical language; a reporter, unless he works for a trade or professional journal, communicates with the mass public in words that the average person readily understands. He has neither the time nor patience to devote to technical discourses.

If you apply the following rules of thumb you will find it easier to deal with the press: make your story simple and nontechnical, and try to be factual yet interesting. Many members of the press corps are over-worked and the majority have to meet daily deadlines. Everyone in Washington has a story to tell; if your story is factual and interesting (with a touch of drama) you will get a chance to tell it.

In order that there will be no misunderstandings between you and the press, establish the rules of the game at the beginning and make sure both you and the reporter understand them. If you do not want to be quoted, tell the interviewer that you wish to go off the record. If you have doubts about the reputation of the reporter, then check him out; some members of the press are known to change the rules in midstream. If this is the case with your interviewer, you will find that his reputation will follow him.

The press corps reflects our social fiber; some are capable and trust-worthy, while others leave much to be desired. Some check their sources out in a professional manner while others simply regurgitate someone's press release in its entirety. Deal only with those who meet your needs and standards. The Washington press corps is a large community—it offers something for everyone.

How to Prepare a Press Release

A press release can often prove to be an important vehicle for commu-nicating with the press. It must do more than merely tell your story; it must do it in an interesting fashion. The Washington press corps is inundated with press releases; thousands of groups, organizations, and government agencies bombard the press daily with their press releases. Thus, the competition for the press's attention can be keen; your press release must be an eye-catcher.

In preparing your press release, there are several rules that you should follow to help make your release more interesting than those of the competition. Among other things, keep your release accurate and to the point. You should also:

Start out with an interesting, current story.

Include dates, figures, and other data (but keep it simple).

Address the release whenever possible to a specific individual (by name) within the news organization.

Keep the release to two or three pages.

Include copies of documents that you want the press to review.

When distributing the release, it is important for you to employ some of the vehicles that ensure it will reach the press. Make copies available to the National Press Club and other known watering holes of the press. Employ some of Washington's press services; these will deliver or wire your release to several hundred news sources. You could also ask congressional staffers to distribute it to their contacts in the press; or approach syndicated columnists. In addition you can call a press conference.

Getting the word out can take many forms; however, it is important that you concentrate most of your efforts on those sources that may have an interest in your story. Do not waste valuable time and money on the shotgun approach; it rarely pays off unless the news is novel or hot. Unless your story has mass appeal, the press will pay scant attention.

Thus, before forwarding your release to the press, make sure that it is juicy. Even the most boring of subjects can be presented in an interesting manner. The news reports that daily inundate our lives are sufficient indicia of this. Thus, when reviewing your release at the final stage, see if it is easily understandable and sufficiently broad to appeal to a mass audience. Direct it at the emotional level. It should be to the point and in tune with current trends in the news media.

Do not, however, limit yourself to the mass media. There are numerous professional and trade publications that reach specialized, but nevertheless important, audiences. In addition, all of the major television networks have their own news bureaus. If you feel your material has sufficient mass appeal, it may prove of interest to those sources. There are also hundreds of newsletter services in Washington which can be valuable vehicles for your press releases. For a detailed listing of Washington's correspondents, check the *Congressional Directory* which lists all those journalists who have been accredited to the press galleries of Congress.

However, the press will in most cases pay little attention to your release unless it carries news of national interest. Since few releases meet this criterion, give your release a novel twist to ensure that it stands out. Present your positions and story in jargon that is both understandable and of interest to the mass-media audience. Washington's press corps, like the society it reflects, is taken by the trendy and novel. News, if presented in a dramatic fashion and flavored with mass appeal, will often bring out the press. Not all news is fit to print, especially when it is stale.

The press, however, is only a vehicle; a medium that can be employed by both you and your opponents. It can be biased, yet is not easily manipulated. The Washington press corps is cynical and inquisitive, but it can often serve as a vehicle for transmitting your story to the executive and Congress.

Role of the Press Conference

There are hundreds of press conferences in Washington daily; every group in town will call a press conference at least once. Few of these, however, attract the attention of the press; many go unattended save for their sponsors. The success of a press conference will depend in large part on your ability to contact the right members of the media and present them with information that is newsworthy. Washington's press corps works on a tight schedule; only newsworthy conferences will bring them out.

Whenever possible, have a celebrity or a well-known member of Congress attend or speak at your conference. The cameras will be there to cover and report on their activities. Washington lives by theatrics; drama and celebrities bring out the cameras.

In getting the word out on your press conference, you can employ several channels. The Associated Press (AP) and the United Press International (UPI) are two traditional and reliable vehicles. Congressional and press contacts can also prove of value. When selecting a site for your conference, select one that is readily accessible to the press; in addition, remember that the best time to hold a conference is in the morning. Avoid late afternoon conferences because the press must meet its deadlines and few of its members will attend.

Also remember that the press corps is comprised largely of men and women who take their jobs seriously. Treat them in a professional manner. Blatant flattery will often get you nowhere and may only serve to irritate some of them: gratuities will fare even worse.

Large corporations often retain the services of expensive public-relations firms; occasionally, you may find it necessary to retain the services of a less-expensive public-relations firm. However, the majority of the tasks for which these firms are retained can often be performed in-house. Many members of the press view these firms with suspicion. Often you will serve your interest better if you represent yourself.

You can easily disseminate your own press releases; it takes little or no skill to contact the press for a conference. A do-it-yourself approach can often serve to enhance your credibility; it makes you come across as being sincere. No one can present your case better than you; all you need are the necessary tools.

Handling Television Interviews

The television news media differs from the traditional press in large part because of the medium itself and the people who operate it—television news has a show-business quality about it. However, you can handle it provided you understand how it functions.

There are several pointers to keep in mind when dealing with television news (some of these also apply to radio news). These are as follows.

Be prepared. Study carefully what you want to say and how you want to say it; you have only a few minutes (if not seconds) to make your point.

Be prompt. In fact, be there well ahead of the scheduled time (even if the interview will be taped) to familiarize yourself with the environment and meet the interviewer.

Be flexible. Do not be surprised if you receive a telephone call at the last minute as regards your appearance.

Cite cases. Illustrate your position with several interesting cases; these also come in handy to clarify technical subject matter.

Avoid brief answers. When possible, give detailed explanations to your interviewer's questions; cite data and studies as these will lend greater authority and legitimacy to your position.

Take the initiative. Do not rely on the interviewer to guide you. Remember that you may be on for only a few minutes; take your best shots.

Do not be afraid. Concentrate on your host and answer his questions with clarity. If you are not sure of your answer, do not be afraid to say so; no one is an expert in all fields. Be frank and avoid evasive tactics; the latter will make you appear insincere.

Be courteous. Politely make your point and rely on your facts and data.

Do not fill dead air time. This is the host's problem; it is not your responsibility to fill it.

Watch the show. Try to watch the program in advance of your appearance. You will get a feel for the host, the type of material covered, and also the type of clothing to wear.

Anyone who wants to have an impact on today's society must understand the press. Bear in mind, however, that this is simply a medium; it suffers from all the human frailties we find in society at large. The best way to deal with the press is to know your facts, be prepared to cite data in support of your position, and present your position in an interesting and entertaining manner.

6

How to Deal with the Regulators

A U.S. Senate study of the federal regulatory process found that agency licensing and rate-making proceedings averaged more than two years; while enforcement actions averaged more than three years, and completed investigations took longer than one year to reach the administrative hearing stage. The Senate study also confirmed that federal regulation was costly. The cost was passed on to consumers in terms of higher prices; for example, fifty cents of every dollar spent by the average family on prescription drugs was directly attributed to regulation.

Regulation has increasingly become complex and mammoth; it impacts on every aspect of our lives. There are now more than 100 regulatory agencies in Washington. These are staffed by more than 100,000 men and women and have annual budgets in the billions of dollars. Knowing how to deal with federal regulation has become a question of survival for the average citizen; understanding the regulatory process is essential.

How Regulation Works

The federal regulators play a role that by far exceeds their numbers. They have an effect on the daily decision-making process of government at all levels, and the social, political, and economic gains and losses of most segments of our society. Regulatory agencies affect how businessmen and consumers interact with each other, how educational institutions select and train their student bodies, and how the legal environment operates. They affect what we eat and wear; and how and where we work.

The regulatory agencies, however, are not uniform; they differ in both structure and jurisdiction. Generally, the regulators fall under one of two categories: those that are headed by a single administrator; and those headed by a commission. The former are found in the executive branch, while the latter often operate outside the executive and legislative branches of government. The Federal Aviation Administration (FAA) of the Department of Transportation is an example of an agency headed by a single administrator. The Interstate Commerce Commission (ICC), the Federal Trade Commission (FTC), the Securities and Exchange Commission (SEC), and the Federal Communications Commission (FCC) are examples of agencies headed by commissions.

Regulation itself takes on one of two forms: *traditional regulation;* and *new regulation*. The former refers to the regulation of specific, identifiable industries. For example, the SEC has specific jurisdiction over the nation's securities industry. New regulation, however, cuts across industry lines. For example, the jurisdiction and regulations of the Occupational Safety and Health Administration (OSHA) encompass both large and small businesses. They are not directed at any one industry or problem. Whereas the objective of traditional regulation is often to safeguard the public from corporate predatory practices, that of new regulation is to safeguard the public's health and welfare, and ensure the safety of workers in industry.

The regulators secure compliance with their rules and regulations through a number of different vehicles. The more common of these are the powers to make rates, to license, and to enact environmental-safety guidelines and product-safety guidelines. They also use their powers to require financial disclosures, limit or expand the scope of privacy, enact health and welfare standards, and investigate corporations and individuals.

Equally important, however, has been the ability of the federal regulators to survive and grow in the face of efforts to reduce regulation. The federal watchdogs have been able to survive because they have powerful allies in the political establishment; this support has come from both liberal and conservative groups. Although corporate America is publicly opposed to regulation, it favors those watchdogs that help it maintain a strong hold on the economy. The legal establishment views regulation as a source of endless litigation, and millions of dollars in legal fees. Thus, calls for regulatory reform have resulted only in cosmetic changes.

The legal basis for the federal regulatory fiber lies in the Commerce Clause of the United States Constitution.[1] The Commerce Clause empowers Congress to "regulate commerce with foreign Nations and among the several states." Congress established the regulatory agencies; it also gave them broad mandates to control the daily activities of the private sector. The watchdogs have jurisdiction to both prescribe and enforce rules and regulations; they are policeman, prosecutor, and judge. The federal regulators have become the fourth branch of government.

How to be Heard by the Regulators

The White House is often instrumental in the selection of an agency's head. Under federal law, the President selects the heads of the single-administrator regulatory agencies. The President also appoints and selects the chairpersons of the independent regulatory commissions. Further, he can remove the heads of the commissions in those instances where they have demonstrated inefficiency, neglect of duty, or malfeasance in office. However, few heads of agencies have been removed for being inefficient, inept, or dishonest.

Although under law the heads of the regulatory agencies are selected by the President, it is the industries that are the kingmakers. Working through congressional committees and the President's staff, industries will often block the selection or appointment of an agency head that is not of their choosing. Industries offer public testimony and evidence at congressional hearings in opposition to an unwanted confirmation of a candidate. However, if you coordinate your efforts with those of other groups, you can also influence the selection of a candidate for an agency post. The key to influencing an appointment often lies in how well you coordinate your efforts and orchestrate the opposition.

More than the White House, it is Congress that plays the key role in the selection of the heads of the independent commissions. Through its power to advise and consent, Congress can easily block the selection of a President's candidate. This highly political selection process ensures that the commission posts are often filled by individuals who have:

Rendered past political service to the President.

Gained powerful support from groups in the industry they will regulate.

Lost other political jobs and are rewarded with an agency post (for example, a congressman who has lost his bid for reelection).

Proven themselves to be staunch party loyalists.

Gained the support of powerful congressional patriarchs.

Been personal friends of the President.

No President in the last fifty years has appointed (or reappointed) an agency head without first seeking the approval of both Congress and the constituencies that the agency regulates. In Washington, the regulated exert a strong veto over who will regulate them; presidential power has its limits in the regulatory area. As a result, the heads of the federal regulatory agencies have often been individuals who are politically safe. The typical agency head is an individual who will not make any waves. However, even when confirmed, an agency head must be responsive to the political environment. He must be attuned to subtle political pressure which can come from both the White House staff and congressional committees with oversight jurisdiction over his agency. Both the executive branch and Congress exert a measure of control over an agency's appropriations.

Before an agency's budget reaches Congress, it is reviewed and often revised by the Office of Management and Budget (OMB). It is through OMB's budgetary knife that the executive branch exerts influence over the agency's policies. Further, all new congressional appropriations must be approved by the President. This serves to give the executive additional leverage over the agency's decision-making process. The need for Presidential approval of an agency's upper-level staffing gives the executive influence over who the agency's decision makers will be; the executive can thus be important in influencing an agency's policies.

Because congressional committees oversee and review all agency budgetary requests, members of Congress and also influential committee staffers affect an agency's decision making; they can assist you in swaying an agency's policies. The news media can also be of value; by airing your opposition to a particular policy, it presents the agency with the threat of congressional inquiries and hearings. Hearings by congressional committees can serve as vehicles for reviewing and scrutinizing an agency's policies. In the final analysis, influencing an agency's actions will rest on your understanding of the regulatory process and a willingness to exert pressure when the need arises.

Scope of an Agency's Powers

Every agency's jurisdiction rests on the organic legislation that created it. The courts, however, have broadly defined an agency's substantive mandate; for example, they have allowed the FTC to enjoin a broad range of unfair trade practices, leaving the question of what is an unfair trade practice largely to the FTC's staff. Agencies also have a broad range of tools they can employ to ensure compliance with their authority, and the courts have proven reluctant to restrict this authority.

An agency's enabling statutes authorize it to engage in many activities but they do not compel it to act. Congress has delegated to the regulators jurisdiction over both the subject matter and the type of activity they regulate. The legislature has also delegated the regulators broad powers to enforce their rules and regulations. How and when an agency proceeds have largely been left, by Congress and the courts, to the discretion of the regulators. The traditional approach has been to "leave it to the experts."

Agencies exert both formal and informal powers. They ensure compliance with their rules and regulations through a series of actions. Among these are the issuance of press releases, advisory opinions, and/or industry guidelines and procedures. They may investigate an individual, corporation, or an entire industry, or hold formal administrative (triallike) hearings. They can file a civil action or refer an investigation to the Department of Justice for criminal prosecution.

Agency prosecutorial, rule-making, and adjudicatory powers have not been well defined; the regulators thus enjoy discretionary authority. This has unfortunately led to agency abuses. In an era of regulation, it is imperative that you understand the scope of an agency's powers.

How Agency Investigations Are Handled

The regulators are empowered to conduct both formal and informal investigations. Some of these result in civil or administrative action, while others (the minority) are referred to the Department of Justice for criminal prosecution.

At the commencement of every investigation, the agency's staff will review the information they have in their files. The staff can also request the target of an investigation to provide additional information, and ask to meet with the target or his representatives. Once an investigation becomes formal, the agency's staff has power (if authorized by the agency head) to issue administrative subpoenas. The staff may also visit the suspect's place of business (though in some cases they must have a search warrant).

An agency's investigatory powers, however, are circumscribed by constitutional and statutory safeguards. While the courts have allowed the agencies broad rule-making powers, they have limited the investigative jurisdiction of the agencies. The IRS is only authorized to investigate tax-related infractions; the SEC is authorized to police only the securities industry. An agency can commence a formal investigation whenever its staff finds that its rules and regulations have been violated. It has no power to investigate infractions that fall outside its statutory jurisdiction. Since each agency guards its turf zealously, other regulators will often prove reluctant to trespass. (Figure 6–1 lists relevant criteria considered by federal agencies on investigations.)

The motivations behind agency investigations differ, as do the objectives. Some investigations are guided by an agency's need to justify its daily existence; others by a need to impress upon Congress and the public the need for additional appropriations. Occasionally, the objective of an investigation may be to discredit critics or political opponents. Regardless of what prompts an investigation, at its conclusion, an agency

A. The staff considers the following matters in an investigation.
   1. Amount of investor losses
   2. Number of public complaints
   3. Nature of securities dealt with
   4. Firm's principal activities
   5. Type of customers
   6. Employees
   7. Selling practices
   8. Reputation of firm's principals
   9. Existence, or lack of any corrective action taken by the firm to prevent future violations
   10. Nature of relief, if any, given to aggrieved customers
   11. Whether firm was cooperative with staff in the investigation of the violations found
   12. The adverse effects upon the firm of the publicity generated by the commission hearing
   13. Whether the violations found involve a new theory or interpretation of the securities laws or involve provisions seldom enforced before
   14. Recommendations of the National Association of Securities Dealers (NASD) or national securities exchanges
   15. Age and health of firm's principals
   16. Losses already suffered by the firm
   17. Whether violations were due to a justifiable mistake or an honest belief that the law was being abided
   18. Whether reasonable inquiries were made to ascertain the facts, which would have prevented or limited the violations
B. The staff often rejects the following arguments put forth by respondents in mitigation of their violations.
   1. Reliance on advice of counsel or accountants
   2. Failure to obtain advice of counsel or accountants
   3. Ignorance or lack of knowledge by the firm's principals that employees were violating the law
   4. Inexperience of the firm's principals in acting as broker–dealers

Figure 6–1. Relevant Criteria Considered in Agency Investigations

can do one or more of the following: bring an administrative action; bring civil action; refer the matter to the Department of Justice for criminal prosecution; or take no action at all and close the investigation.

Although some of Washington's establishment lawyers scare their clients with the agency bogeyman, few cases result in criminal prosecution. A small number, however, do result in administrative and civil proceedings. The latter often culminate in a consent agreement. The overwhelming majority of an agency's investigations die within the agency.

Some federal agencies are authorized to conduct on-site inspections. FDIC inspectors can visit and examine the records of federally insured banks. The SEC's staff can likewise visit and inspect the records of broker–dealers. The objective of on-site visits is to deter infractions. These inspections can spark a formal investigation, although in practice very few do.

If you should be the target of such visitation, request that your attorney be present. You may also request the agency's staff to first obtain a search warrant. You should try to determine the purpose for the visitation; it may be part of a larger agency investigation.

When confronted with an agency investigation, make an effort to ascertain:

Whether you are a target.

What sparked the investigation.

What infractions are involved.

Whether the investigation is formal or informal.

Whether the investigation is a fishing expedition.

Who the agency's witnesses are.

To assist in an investigation you should do the following.

Place an FOIA request with the agency (unless the investigation is formal, the agency will have to comply in part or whole with your request).

Review your case (witnesses, documents) with a lawyer.

Prepare for the interview with the agency's staff.

You may ask your lawyer to accompany you to an investigatory interview. Be sure to take good notes; if the case should make its way to court, the notes may serve you well. Further, be sure to weigh the impact of the investigation on your business or career. If you suspect you are the target of the investigation, start to prepare your defense as early as possible; take active steps to minimize your losses. Have a positive attitude and be aggressive should the need arise.

The following are some sample preliminary questions a suspect witness will be asked in a federal investigation.

Full name

Use of any other names

Date and place of birth (if foreign born, date and place of naturalization)
Home address and telephone number or numbers
Any other homes, apartments, or telephone numbers

Telephone credit card

Business address and telephone numbers, and the names of all businesses located at business premises

Position held at present firm

Schooling (major subjects, degrees, dates) and military service (honorable discharge?)

Brief résumé of positions held since school, with dates

Officer or director of any publicly held companies

Location of all securities brokerage accounts and bank accounts (checking, savings, safe deposit boxes)

Location of all real property

Congress has deferred broad investigatory powers to the regulators. An agency can direct an individual or corporation to file periodic reports; request answers to specific questions; request or direct an individual to testify before its staff; and subpoena documentary evidence. Although the courts object to fishing expeditions by agencies, they have proven reluctant to interfere with their investigatory authority. However, the regulators are not beyond the law. The courts will not permit them to infringe upon an individual's constitutional rights.

In preparing a legal challenge to an agency's investigation, one should consider whether the investigation was:

Within the scope of the agency's congressional mandate.

Conducted pursuant to some legitimate agency objective.

Conducted in a manner that intimidated a witness.

Authorized by the appropriate head(s) of the agency.

Conducted in accord with the agency's rules and regulations.

Conducted in accord with the latest judicial decisions.

The burden of demonstrating that an agency's staff acted improperly, or beyond its statutory jurisdiction, rests with the target of its inquiry. He must convince a court that the agency's requests were unreasonable and/or overbroad, or that its staff conducted the investigation in an unlawful manner. An agency's staff will often shy away when faced with a determined member of the public; the judicial arena is not to their liking. Fear of adverse publicity and the in-house red tape often militate against confrontation. The threat of judicial action can also serve as leverage when dealing with agency staff. However, before you take on the staff, be sure that you stand on solid ground.

Targets of federal investigations have an adequate arsenal of legal rights, and also the media and the courts to ensure that those rights are respected. If you feel that an agency's staff has infringed upon your legal rights, remember that you do have recourse. You, or your lawyer, can turn to one or more of the following for assistance.

The federal courts

The news media

Members of Congress, or congressional committees (especially those with jurisdiction over the agency)

Civil-rights, professional/trade, or consumer groups

Head of the executive department (for example, to the Secretary of the Department of Transportation if you have a complaint against the FAA)

Occasionally, an agency's request or subpoena for documents or testimony may go beyond the scope of its jurisdiction; it may be unreasonable, oppressive, overbroad, or costly to comply with. In such a case, you have one of two available options; you can take active steps to oppose it, or refuse to comply and let the agency itself take steps to enforce it.

Should you decide to oppose an agency's request, remember that taking active steps to do so can be expensive; it may also anger the agency staff. Few individuals or corporations have the requisite resources and time to exhaust an agency's internal remedies and then turn to the courts. There are, however, advantages to forcing an agency to go to court. It can help you:

Conserve valuable resources for the ongoing investigation and future prosecutions (administrative, civil, or criminal).

Use the judicial arena (at the agency's expense) to publicly air your grievances.

Place the burden on the agency to convince the court that compliance with its request is both reasonable and lawful.

Delay an agency's investigation by several months, since its efforts must now be directed at the coming judicial proceedings.

You may be told by some of the establishment lawyers that being tough with a regulator will get you nowhere; that it will merely serve to toughen the regulator's reserve to get you. What these lawyers often will not tell you is that they and the agency's staff are sometimes on very friendly terms. Washington's legal establishment enjoys a close relationship with the federal bureaucracy; its livelihood depends in large part upon the good will of the regulators. The establishment lawyer can ill afford to alienate the regulator; a client's interests can sometimes suffer.

In most cases, the regulators will shy away from a tough battle; they delight in the genteel art of paper warfare. They stand to gain little from confrontation with a determined opponent. You will be a winner if you play tough when your rights are infringed.

Know Your Rights

The federal bureaucracy must comply with both constitutional and statutory safeguards. An overzealous staff, however, often forgets this; thus, it is important that you be aware of your rights. You cannot be directed to respond to a question if its answer can serve to incriminate you, or result in evidence that can be used against you in a criminal prosecution. Fifth Amendment safeguards apply to both verbal and written communications; the privilege extends to citizens and noncitizens alike.

An agency can circumvent this privilege by asking the Department of Justice to grant a witness immunity. The regulators themselves lack this authority. However, a grant of immunity from criminal prosecution does not preclude an agency from bringing civil or administrative action at some future date; nor does the fact that a witness may face the loss of his job or peer ridicule serve as a defense against an agency's request for documents or testimony.

All witnesses in a government investigation have a right to be accompanied to the interview by counsel of their choosing. They have a right to be represented by an attorney at all stages of the investigation. During the interview an agency's staff must inform a witness that any testimony or evidence he gives can be used against him in any future criminal, civil, or administrative action. Indigents can request a local public defender's office to represent them, but an agency is under no legal obligation to appoint counsel for indigents.[2] The right to counsel comes into play only in criminal investigations; since a regulatory agency does not have any criminal investigative or prosecutorial powers, it is not obligated by law to provide a witness with counsel.

An agency investigation is often embarrassing and damaging to an individual business and reputation. Even when an agency chooses to keep its findings confidential, all or part of them may become public (at the conclusion of its investigation) as the result of an FOIA request. You should always ask the staff to inform you of any FOIA requests for your records or testimony, so that you may be able to bring a reverse-FOIA action to stop (in part or in whole) their release.

How Agencies Make Rules

Regulatory agencies act as quasi-legislative bodies. They issue and interpret new rules and regulations. However, before an agency can propose a new rule, it must first consult with the public and specifically the industry it regulates. The public must be given an opportunity to comment on an agency's proposed rules. These public comments can be in the form of written or oral testimony. If you should be opposed to an agency's proposed rule, make the agency aware of your objections. Do not wait until the rule is adopted; that will be too late.

An agency also has the power to issue interpretations of its old rules which serve as guides for both its staff and the industry it regulates. An agency's interpretations can take one of several forms: press releases; formal rulings; and rulings by one of its administrative law judges. As with the making of new rules, the agency is required to first solicit public comments. Should you be opposed to a proposed interpretation, you have the right to submit written or verbal testimony. An agency's interpretations are not always binding—they can be challenged in court. The latter is the final arbitrator. The courts will occasionally differ with the regulators, but in the majority of cases a court will be reluctant to overturn an agency's decisions.

An agency is also authorized to repeal or amend its old rules. To do this it must first publish its intentions in the *Federal Register*. The notice must announce the proposed rule change and invite the public to comment. Any interested member of the public can submit written or oral testimony. Once an agency has made a decision, it must then proceed to publish the proposed or modified rule at least thirty days before its adoption. Comments are solicited once again and members of the public can submit testimony. If you are interested in keeping abreast of an agency's rule making, stay in touch with its staff. Request that you be placed on its mailing list, and check the *Federal Register* periodically.

How Administrative Hearings Operate

On occasion, an agency's investigations will result in some form of administrative action (hearing). This triallike proceeding is employed by an agency to resolve disputed questions of fact, and to determine whether any of its rules or regulations have been violated. These quasi-judicial proceedings are heard by an agency administrative law judge. During the administrative hearing, the agency's staff and the defense are afforded equal opportunity to present testimony and evidence, and to cross-examine each other's witnesses. At the conclusion of the administrative hearing, the judge will either render his decision or take the case under advisement. The decision can be appealed to the head(s) of the agency or the courts.

Administrative proceedings are governed by specific provisions of the Administrative Procedure Act.[3] In addition, each agency has enacted its own procedures for the conduct of an administrative hearing. These can be found in the *Federal Register* and the *Federal Code of Regulations*. Administrative proceedings are often open to the public and are conducted in accord with the evidentiary rules that govern federal civil proceedings.

The testimony and evidence presented at these hearings is open for public inspection. These hearings can often serve as discovery vehicles for litigants; the testimony and evidence introduced at them can be used in a civil proceeding. In those instances where the proceedings are closed, an FOIA request may gain you access to the evidence presented at the hearing.

All administrative hearings commence with a written (formal) complaint filed by the agency's staff against a person or corporation (respondent). Once the agency has filed its administrative complaint, the respondent is then afforded an opportunity to file an answer. Discovery between the two sides then follows. The administrative law judge may hold a pretrial conference; he will also set the hearing date. These administrative proceedings are less formal than a civil trial. The agency is represented by one or more of its staff attorneys, while the respondent may be represented by counsel or choose to represent himself. At the end of the hearing, both sides will have an opportunity to submit written briefs and proposed findings of fact.

A respondent has a right to appeal an adverse decision. The appeal must be directed to the head(s) of the agency. The respondent and the agency's staff are afforded a second opportunity to submit written and oral arguments. The head of the agency will then, after having reviewed the case, render his own decision. Reversing an administrative law judge's decision is the exception rather than the norm. If the respondent takes exception with this, he has a right to appeal the case to a U.S. court of appeals.

Administrative hearings can be time-consuming. Some cases have been known to take several years before a decision is rendered; most cases, however, are disposed of sooner. Delay may prove advantageous to a party that does not want a speedy resolution of the case.

Your Right to Judicial Review

All regulatory agency actions are open to judicial scrutiny. The judicial role is twofold:

First: to determine if the agency acted within its delegated powers.

Second: to ensure that the agency has not abused its discretionary powers.

A challenge to an agency's rules, decision-making, or administrative hearings can take one of several forms: it can have constitutional and/or statutory basis; or it may question the agency's interpretation of an applicable rule or statute. Courts are also called upon to consider whether an agency has acted unreasonably or capriciously. Challenges in this area often focus on how the agency handled its rule-making or interpretations, its investigations, or the respondent's appeal; or how it complied with its own rules, regulations, and statutes at large.

An appeal from an agency's decision must be brought before the filing period has expired. If a timely appeal is not filed, the agency's order becomes final and self-executing. As a rule, requests for judicial review are granted with little difficulty, but the courts are reluctant to overturn an agency's decisions. Your appeal should thus focus on one or more of the following.

Agency's statutes, rules, and/or regulations.

Scope of the agency's discretion.

Expertise of the agency.

Likelihood that there was an abuse of power by the agency.

Alternative methods available to the court to resolve the dispute.

Judicial holdings in similar cases.

Before filing an appeal, remember to first exhaust all of the internal administrative remedies. The doctrine of exhaustion will bar any premature court review of your case. However, the doctrine will not come into play if you are appealing a final adverse order, or if the agency chooses to enforce its own order in court. Before embarking on a judicial review of your case, remember that it can be costly and time-consuming; in addition, the odds are against the appellant. Employ this route only as your last resort.

Regulation Can Be a Thorn

Federal regulation has proven to be both costly and slow. It took the FCC more than thirty years to resolve a dispute between a radio station in New York City and one of its competitors in New Mexico. However, some persons and corporations have employed this snail-like process to their advantage. They have used it to frustrate the efforts of both their competitors and the regulators. The numerous rules and regulations of the many government agencies are often at odds with one another. For example, some OSHA rules are at odds with those of the U.S. Department of Agriculture. These contradictions can work to your advantage.

The annual cost of regulation runs in the billions of dollars. The private sector alone spends more than $30 billion each year just to comply with federal record-keeping requirements. Regardless of whether one is a proponent or opponent of federal regulation, the inescapable conclusion is that regulation gives rise to sundry legal problems; the costs being borne by the public. Overzealous regulation can also threaten our rights and freedoms. Thus, understanding how the regulatory process works has become, for the public, a first-aid kit for survival.

Notes

1. See, Article I, Section 8 of the United States Constitution.
2. Since a regulatory agency's investigations are noncriminal in nature, even a Public Defender's Office can refuse to provide legal assistance. See, the Administrative Procedure Act, 5 U.S.C. 555b.
3. See, 5 U.S.C. 554–557.

Appendix 6A
Handling an
Administrative
Proceeding

The following are key steps to consider in an agency hearing.

I. Prehearing stage
    A. Outline of charges
        1. Allegations should be set forth in sufficient detail to permit respondent to file a meaningful answer.
        2. Review allegations for ambiguities or inadvertent errors.
    B. Motion for default
        1. Request for default order can be made prior to commencement of hearing if a respondent has failed to file notice of appearance or answer.
        2. Effort must first be made to determine whether the respondent has actually received notice of the proceeding and if he intends a defense.
    C. Prehearing motions
        1. Motions must set forth the specific relief requested, the material facts to be considered, and the reason why the request should be granted.
        2. A brief of the points and authorities relied upon must always accompany the motion.
        3. The respondent often has five to ten days within which to answer.
    D. Negotiations explored at the prehearing stage
    E. Prehearing conference with hearing examiner
        1. If informal negotiations are to no avail, consider requesting a formal prehearing conference.
        2. Request should be specific as to matters to be considered.
II. Administrative Hearing
    A. Basics
        1. File notice of appearance with hearing examiner.
        2. File motions.
        3. Be prepared to make an opening statement in sufficient detail to acquaint the hearing examiner with specific information relating to the case.
    B. Introduction of testimony on direct
        1. Ask witness to state name, address, and occupation.

        2. Put witness at ease by a few preliminary questions that lend themselves to ready answers.

        3. Elicit testimony through short, simple questions.

        4. Be certain that the answers are clear and responsive to the questions.

    C. Introduction and use of documents

        1. Permit respondent to examine the documents that are to be offered prior to the commencement of the hearing.

        2. Refrain from burdening record with documents that are simply repetitious of testimony that is unchallenged.

        3. Identify and offer into evidence only the relevant portion of a document.

    D. Use of cross-examination

        1. Limit cross-examination to specific areas.

        2. Insist on direct and responsive answers.

    E. Rules of evidence

        1. Hearsay evidence, inadmissible in judicial proceedings, may be accepted in an administrative proceeding.

        2. Reasons for objections should be stated succinctly.

III.   Posthearing steps

    A. Procedural steps to consider

        1. Filings of proposed findings of fact, conclusions of law, and brief must be considered.

        2. Proposed findings must encompass salient facts.

        3. Page references to transcript of testimony or to exhibits.

    B. Posthearing brief

        1. Be clear and direct.

        2. Quality rather than quantity should be criterion.

        3. Reply brief may be filed in reply to opponent's arguments.

        4. Application for extension of time should be filed as soon as possible; it must show good cause for granting extension.

Appendix 6B
Sources Reviewed by Government Investigators

Whenever federal investigators conduct an investigation, they turn to a variety of sources. Counsel and his client should review those sources when preparing for an interview with federal investigators. By the time of the interview, the investigators will either have or are in the process of contacting the following sources.

I. Governmental sources available to investigators
   A. IRS
      1. Tax returns
      2. Information obtainable from intelligence sources
   B. Department of Justice
      1. Organized-crime files (lists, summaries, and detailed data)
      2. Contacts with assistant U.S. attorneys who have handled cases involving particular individuals
      3. Immigration and Naturalization Service
   C. Department of State (passport information: the application, type of data, the correspondence, other)
   D. Social Security
   E. Coast Guard
   F. Department of Commerce
   G. CIA
   H. FBI
   I. Post Office Department
      1. Post-office cases
      2. Mail covers
   J. Agencies with which suspect may have had contact
      1. Federal Trade Commission
      2. Small Business Administration
      3. Defense Department (contracts)
      4. SEC
      5. Others
   K. Congressional committees
      1. Hearings
      2. Indices (as published in hearings volumes and the committees' own detailed index systems)
   L. Court records

M. Real-estate records
  1. Index system of grantors and grantees
  2. Examination of documents for address of buyers and sellers, details of transactions, stamp-tax indication of prices, and identity of settlement company
N. Marriages, wills, and court records
O. Police records, automobile registration, and operators license data
P. Information regarding imprisoned persons
  1. Visitors to prisoner (from warden)
  2. Telephone calls made from prison (the telephone company)
Q. Data procurable from state and foreign agencies
  1. State and local governments
  2. Foreign countries

II. Data from directories
  A. City directories
  B. Martindale Hubbell
  C. Trade or professional directories
  D. Congressional directories
  E. *Directory of Directors* (by individuals and companies)
  F. *Who's Who*
    1. *Who's Who in America*
    2. Regional *Who's Who* (south and southwest, east, et cetera)
    3. *Who's Who in Commerce and Industry*

III. Telephone company as source
  A. Telephone directories
  B. Cross-index directories
  C. Telephone toll slips
  D. Opening account cards
  E. Installation records
  F. Data-processing center (for names of subscribers of phones no longer operating)
  G. Obtaining copies of basic telegrams referred in toll charges

IV. Other sources
  A. Airline companies' records of tickets and charges
  B. Hotel records (room and other charges; names of guests; records of local and toll telephone calls)
  C. Bank records
    1. Opening account cards
    2. Loan application (loan records, collateral cards)
    3. Safe-vault records and entry cards
    4. Checks issued (including cancellations, showing bank used by payees)

    5. Checks deposited

    6. Correspondence files

D. Brokerage records

    1. Clearing-corporation final-reconciliation records

    2. Exchange and National Association of Securities Dealers (NASD) Files (specialist and registered trader reports

    3. Opening account cards

    4. Customer's statements

    5. Correspondence files

    6. Ledger sheets showing transactions

    7. Firms' automated-surveillance and record-keeping data

    8. Identification of registered representative

    9. Interview regarding opening of accounts

    10. Trading questionnaires

E. Credit agencies and credit-card organizations

    1. Diners Clubs, American Express, Hilton, et cetera

    2. Dunn and Bradstreet Reports

    3. Bishop Service

    4. Proudfoot Reports

    5. Worldwide Information Service

    6. Exchange Firms Information Corporation

    7. Local credit agencies

F. Newspaper and periodical data

    1. *Funk & Scott Index of Corporate Items* in newspapers and periodicals

    2. *New York Times Index*

    3. *Wall Street Journal Index*

    4. *Industrial Arts Index*

    5. *Fortune Magazine Index*

    6. *New Yorker, Fairchild Publications,* et cetera

    7. Newspaper morgues and their indices

    8. S&P Corporation Records

    9. *Moody's*

G. SEC sources

    1. General Index in Docket Section

    2. T&M complaint Section Index

    3. CFD Index of Attorneys, CPAs and Officers and Directors listed in Securities Act Registration A statements

    4. CFD Index (in Regulation A filings)

    5. CFD Index of Section 16 filings (by companies or by individuals)

    6. T&M Broker–Dealer and Investment Adviser Index

    7. Mail and Records Index of Brief Cards

    8. Public Reference Room Index of Individuals Named in SEC Releases

    9. Basic 33 and 34 Act Registration Files (data on officers, finders, underwriters, et cetera)

   10. Importance of data in Attendant Correspondence Files

   11. Transcripts of hearing

   12. Contents of complaint files

   13. 132–3 files

   14. B–D files and I–A files

   15. SV files

   16. Section 16a files

H. Others

    1. Use of persons who are acquainted with individual under investigation (for example, associates and other persons in same business)

    2. Discussions with other government investigators who have worked on cases involving suspect

**Part II
The Institutions and How
They Work**

7 How the Judicial Establishment Works

Prison systems in several dozen states have been under detailed court orders to improve conditions. In one large eastern city, a judge forced officials to provide lodging for thousands of homeless persons. Another judge ordered a university to readmit a star basketball player despite his poor grades.

Americans are a very litigious people; more than half the world's lawyers are found in this country, and on the average, Americans file more than 10 million lawsuits each year. At the center of this legal maze lies the federal judicial establishment. It both leads and guides; it has, some say, extended its reach into the provinces of the executive and legislative branches. How the judicial establishment works should be a matter of interest and concern to the U.S. public.

How the Supreme Court Operates

Section I, Article 3 of the Constitution provides that judicial power is to be vested in the Supreme Court and "in such inferior courts as Congress may from time to time ordain and establish." The U.S. Supreme Court is comprised of a Chief Justice and eight associate justices. Six of its members constitute a quorum. Only attorneys who are members of the Supreme Court bar may practice before it; only the attorneys for the federal government and members of Congress may use its library. The Court's term commences the first Monday in October of each year and continues as long as the business before it requires.

The Supreme Court has broad jurisdiction; its clerks screen some 5,000 petitions per year asking for review of lower-court rulings. Its workload in the last twenty years has seen a doubling of the appeals filed annually. It has jurisdiction over all cases in law and equity arising under the Constitution and also over constitutional laws and treaties. The Court exercises jurisdiction over all:

Cases involving ambassadors, ministers, and consuls.

Cases of admiralty in maritime jurisdiction.

Controversies to which the federal government is a party.

Controversies between two or more states.

Controversies between a state and a citizen of another state.

Controversies between citizens of different states.

Controversies between individuals of the same state, and claims on lands and grants of different states.

Controversies between a state or one of its citizens and a foreign state or its citizens.

The Court also has original jurisdiction over all cases affecting ambassadors, ministers and consuls, and those cases in which a state is a party. It has appellate jurisdiction in all other cases;[1] this was conferred upon it by Congress through legislation. However, Congress has no power to alter the Court's original jurisdiction. The Court also prescribes the rules and procedures that are followed by the lower federal courts. These govern: criminal and civil cases; bankruptcy proceedings; admiralty cases; copyright cases; and appellate proceedings.

Cases normally reach the Supreme Court for the purpose of review in one of two ways: *appeal—as a matter of right; or writ of certiorari—* as a matter of discretion by the Court. Those cases reaching the Court on appeal come from:

State courts, when they declare a federal law or treaty unconstitutional. Also when a state law or constitution is challenged on the ground that it conflicts with the U.S. Constitution or some federal law.

U.S. courts of appeals, if a state law is invalidated, or a federal law is held to be unconstitutional.

U.S. district courts, when a federal statute is held unconstitutional, a special three-judge panel has granted or denied an injunction, or when the federal government is a party to a civil suit.

Other federal courts, such as the Court of Claims, or the Court of Customs and Patent Appeals.

Cases also reach the Court on a writ of certiorari; for this to occur, at least four of the justices must agree to grant a review. Writs are heard from:

State courts, in cases where a substantial federal question is raised, except where the remedy is appeal.

U.S. courts of appeals, where applications or interpretations of federal laws or treaties are involved.

Other federal courts with questions of federal law.

Understanding the Lower Courts

The federal appellate courts are intermediary tribunals that were established by the Congress to relieve the Supreme Court of appeals from the lower federal courts.[2] The appellate courts are divided into eleven judicial circuits, plus the District of Columbia circuit. Each circuit has its own court of appeals; these hear cases in divisions consisting of three judges. The senior judge is the Chief Judge. The circuits and the districts they cover are as follows.

Circuit	*District*
District of Columbia	District of Columbia
First	Maine; New Hampshire; Massachusetts; Rhode Island; Puerto Rico
Second	Vermont; Connecticut; Northern, Eastern, and Western New York
Third	New Jersey; Eastern, Middle, and Western Pennsylvania; Delaware; Virgin Islands
Fourth	Maryland; Northern, and Southern West Virginia; Eastern, and Western Virginia; Eastern, Middle, and Western North Carolina; South Carolina
Fifth	Northern, and Southern Mississippi; Eastern, Middle, and Western Louisiana; Northern, Southern, Eastern, and Western Texas
Sixth	Northern, and Southern Ohio; Eastern, and Western Michigan; Eastern, and Western Kentucky; Eastern, Middle, and Western Tennessee
Seventh	Northern, and Southern Indiana; Northern, Eastern, and Southern Illinois; Eastern, and Western Wisconsin

Eighth	Minnesota; Northern, and Southern Iowa; Eastern and Western Missouri; Eastern, and Western Arkansas; Nebraska; North Dakota; South Dakota
Ninth	Northern, Eastern, Central, and Southern California; Oregon; Nevada; Montana; Eastern, and Western Washington; Idaho; Arizona; Alaska; Hawaii; Territory of Guam
Tenth	Colorado; Wyoming; Utah; Kansas; Eastern, Western, and Northern Oklahoma; New Mexico
Eleventh	Northern, Middle, and Southern Georgia; Northern, Middle, and Southern Florida; Northern, Middle, and Southern Alabama

A Supreme Court justice is assigned to act as Circuit Justice for each circuit. Federal courts of appeals have authority to review all final decisions, and also certain interlocutory decisions from the district courts.[3] These appellate courts are also required to review and enforce the orders of the federal regulatory agencies. Orders of the appellate courts are final, and subject only to discretionary review or appeal to the Supreme Court.

The federal trial courts are known as district courts. These exercise general jurisdiction, and at least one district court is found in each state. There are also district courts for Washington, D.C., and the Commonwealth of Puerto Rico; their jurisdiction corresponds to that of the federal district courts found in the states. Cases in these courts are often heard and decided by only one judge. In some instances, however, three-judge panels can be convened to hear a case.[4] The senior judge acts as a district court's Chief Judge.

District court judges hold their offices during good behavior; for all practical purposes they constitute an oligarchy appointed for life.[5] It has been said by some that it is easier to remove a President from office than a district court judge.

District court cases are reviewed by courts of appeal. However, decisions holding acts of Congress unconstitutional, and injunctive orders from special three-judge district court panels can be appealed directly to the Supreme Court.[6]

Knowing the Specialized Tribunals

Congress has also created a number of specialized courts to deal with different aspects of our society. Appeals from these specialized tribunals are often heard by the Supreme Court. Among the more important of these specialized courts are the: Court of Claims; Court of Customs and Patent Appeals; Court of Military Appeals; and Tax Court. Although these tribunals play an important role in our lives, both the press and the public seem to have relegated them to oblivion. It would serve you well to have some familiarity with their jurisdictions.

Court of Claims

This tribunal has original jurisdiction in cases dealing with claims against the federal government, where the claim is founded upon one of the following:[7] the Constitution; acts of Congress; regulations of the executive branch; or implied contracts with the federal government. The court also has jurisdiction to hear cases that arise out of claims: under construction and supply contracts; by civilian and military personnel; for backpay and retirement pay; and for the refund of federal income and excise taxes.

The Court of Claims can hear cases where the federal government has used, without authorization, an invention covered by a patent; or has infringed on any work protected by a copyright without first obtaining the authorization of its owner.[8] The court is staffed by sixteen trial judges.

Judgments of the court are final and conclusive, unless reviewed by the Supreme Court on a writ of certiorari. The court has national jurisdiction, and a plaintiff can commence his action by filing a lawsuit. Service of process is made on the U.S. Attorney General. Trials are conducted before a judge of the court, often at a location most convenient to the plaintiff and his witnesses. Once a case is tried, both sides have an opportunity to file written briefs with the chief judge of the court and the six associate judges who sit in panels of three.

Court of Customs and Patent Appeals

This tribunal enjoys nationwide jurisdiction. It hears appeals from the Customs Court,[9] Patent and Trademark Office,[10] and the International Trade Commission.[11] It also hears appeals from decisions by the Secretary of Commerce,[12] Secretary of Agriculture,[13] and petitions for extraordinary writs under the Old Writs Act.[14] All of its judgments are final, but they must be reviewed by the Supreme Court on writ of certiorari.

The court is made up of a Chief Judge who is assisted by four associate judges. Most cases are heard in Washington, D.C., but on request they can be heard in other cities.

Customs Court

This court was established as a court of record.[15] It has jurisdiction over cases involving the following.

Civil actions arising under the tariff clause

Classifications, rates, and amounts of duties chargeable

The exclusion of merchandise from entry or delivery under provisions of the custom laws

Refusals to pay a claim for drawback

Civil actions brought by U.S. manufacturers, producers, or wholesalers, pursuant to the Tariff Act

Protests from determinations of the appropriate customs officer under the AntiDumping Act of 1921[16]

The court is made up of a Chief Judge and eight associate judges, no more than five of whom may belong to any one political party. All cases are tried and decided before a single judge; appeals are taken to the Court of Customs and Patent Appeals in Washington. The principal offices of the Customs Court are located in New York City, however it can hear cases arising at other ports of entry.

Court of Military Appeals

This court hears appeals from military court martials. It is the final appellate tribunal for the armed services.[17] The court consists of three judges who are appointed by the President. The court will hear cases certified to it by the Judge Advocate General's Office; The General Counsel of the Department of Transportation, acting for the Coast Guard; or the petitions by convicted felons who have received sentences in excess of one year. Its decisions are final and no further direct review is allowed.

Tax Court

This tribunal tries and adjudicates controversies involving the existence of deficiencies or overpayments in income, estate, gift, or personal holding-company surtaxes.[18] The court also has jurisdiction to redetermine excise taxes and penalties imposed on private foundations by the Internal Revenue Service;[19] and can hear disputes involving $1,500 or less.[20] It can render judgments regarding the qualifications of retirement, pension, profit-sharing, stock, bonus, and bond-purchase plans.

All of its decisions are subject to review by a federal court of appeals, and thereafter the Supreme Court. The court's headquarters are in Washington, D.C., but it can also hear cases in locations more convenient to the taxpayer. Cases are heard by single judges and the federal rules of evidence (applicable in the federal district courts) apply in the course of its trials.

Washington is the home of the federal judicial establishment; here, too, are found an assortment of specialized tribunals. To practice before these courts one must be a member of their bars. Private litigants can also appear before them to represent themselves. In complex litigation, however, it is advised that one consult with attorneys who practice before these courts. These specialized tribunals have gained a reputation for bias toward the government; some attorneys would thus rather litigate disputes of up to $10,000 before the federal district courts.

The federal judiciary, armed with their scriptures and institutions, wield a powerful influence over our daily lives. They often rule their courts like the magnates of feudal England. By necessity, if their abuses are to be curtailed, the public must better understand the federal judicial maze. Like the bureaucracy, they, too, can threaten our freedoms if left unchecked.

Notes

1. See, 20 U.S.C. 1251–1258.
2. See, 28 U.S.C. chapter 3.
3. See, 28 U.S.C. 1291–1292
4. See, 28 U.S.C. 2281–2284.
5. See, 28 U.S.C. 1331–1359 and 1361.
6. See, 28 U.S.C. 1252–1253, and 18 U.S.C. 3731.
7. See, 28 U.S.C. 171 and 1491–1507.
8. See, 28 U.S.C. 1498.
9. See, 28 U.S.C. 1541.
10. See, 28 U.S.C. 1542.
11. See, 28 U.S.C. 1548.
12. See, 28 U.S.C. 1544.
13. See, 28 U.S.C. 1545.
14. See, 28 U.S.C. 1651.

15. See, 28 U.S.C. 251, and 1582–1583.
16. See, 19 U.S.C. 160–171, as amended by 84 Stat. 275.
17. See, 10 U.S.C. 867, 64 Stat. 129, and 82 Stat. 178 and 342.
18. See, 48 Stat. 336.
19. See, 83 Stat. 524.
20. See, 33 Stat. 733.

8

Dealing with the Executive

The White House staff is more than a glorified correspondence section of the Executive Office of the President. It is one of the more important agencies found within the Executive Office. These agencies play an important role in running the federal apparatus and in formulating policy.

Understanding how the agencies and departments that constitute the Executive Office function, the scope of their powers and jurisdiction, and the in-house political games, can ensure that you will have some form of input in their decision-making processes. It will also ensure that the workings of the Executive Office will become more meaningful.

The Presidency

The Constitution provides that the executive power shall be vested in the President.[1] Together with the Vice-President, he holds office for four years. He is also assisted by a cabinet which advises the President on numerous policy issues. Represented in the cabinet are the heads of the executive departments and also some executive-branch officials who have been accorded cabinet rank. The Vice-President sits in on cabinet meetings, and occasionally other government officials are invited to attend.

The President reigns over a multitude of agencies in addition to the cabinet. Many of these are the creations of legislation enacted in the last seventy years. For example, the Reorganization Act of 1933 transferred some of the federal agencies to the Executive Office;[2] and Executive Order No. 8248 created many of the agencies presently found within the Executive Office. Numerous other statutes and executive orders confer on these agencies and departments both regulatory and quasi-judicial powers.

Executive Departments

The oldest and best known of the executive departments is the Department of State; the newest is the Department of Education. The executive departments have annual budgets in the billions of dollars, and employ large numbers of bureaucrats. The departments also have developed and nurtured powerful constituencies through the annual disbursement of billions of dollars in contracts, grants, programs, studies, and numerous other services. Powerful bureaucrats rule these departments, in alliance with their constituencies, like feudal lords. The executive departments are often components of the Executive Office only in name—their policies and objectives have a momentum of their own. A weak President often exerts little control over these powerful principalities.

At the top of each department is a secretary; he is appointed by the President, with the advice and consent of the Senate, and (at least in name) serves at the pleasure of the President. Under him are found the departmental undersecretaries, who are delegated a number of important positions and tasks within the department. Each departmental secretary is also assisted by at least three assistant secretaries who are assigned specific areas of responsibility. These can range from reviewing and overseeing budgetary concerns to the supervision of departmental programs and contracts.

Each department is divided into several divisions, bureaus, and offices. These, in turn, are headed by a chief or a director. Many of these officials are political appointees with varying expertise. It is the bureaus, however, that are responsible for much of the real work in each department; thus, inquiries on specific problems should be referred to the departmental bureau with responsibility and jurisdiction over the area that concerns you.

You should also be aware that it is the career bureaucrats within these divisions and bureaus who exert the greatest influence on the daily workings of the departments. This is a result of their expertise and knowledge of departmental politics and tasks. These individuals can, in many ways, serve you better than the political appointees. They will be there long after the political appointees have left; they are permanent fixtures.

Occasionally, you may find that your efforts to meet with an assistant secretary or bureau chief are fruitless. Should this occur, contact a member of Congress or one of his key staffers and request that they make an effort to set up an appointment for you. However, this route also carries some risks with it—it can anger the bureaucrats. In the long run, going around the bureaucrats will undermine your short-term gains. If you choose to take the political route, be subtle; do not flaunt your political contacts. Use power wisely—let the bureaucrat know you have it, but employ it with restraint. Even political power and contacts are finite.

The departments are broken down into regional and branch offices which are found in the larger cities. It may prove more economical in time and money to contact one of these local offices with a problem. Turn to headquarters only if you find that the local office is either unwilling or unable to assist you.

When dealing with department officials and staff, remember that courtesy can go a long way. The bureaucrat, like any other person, will appreciate a letter of commendation to his superiors. Further, make it a practice to maintain periodic contacts with those in the bureaucracy. The department bureaucrat often views his job as a thankless endeavor; for him, the public is a demanding and ungrateful master. There is some justification for this view. A semblance of recognition or appreciation for his efforts will serve you well.

White House Staff

The public often associates the Executive Office with the White House staff; they are not the same. The White House staff is only one of the many components of the Executive Office, albeit an important one. It plays a number of important roles. Primarily, it is the President's palace guard. It maintains and coordinates communications between the president and congress (although sometimes it does this poorly). The staff also assists the President in ensuring that the heads of the executive agencies and departments carry out his policies and directives.

The White House staff has grown in size and importance with the expanding role of the presidency. The staff is composed of personal aides and assistants to the President; its great power rests on its proximity to the chief executive. It is the White House staff that most often attracts the ire of the public; it is also the agency that handles the President's communications with the public. However, the news media has created the erroneous impression that the White House staff is all powerful. You should not forget that the other executive agencies also exert great powers; thus, if you have a problem, contact the agency with specific jurisdiction over that area.

The White House staff, however, is more than the President's public-relations office; it exerts varying powers. Under a weak chief executive, it can play an important role in the selection of high-level government officials; it can also play an important role in decisions affecting the location of military bases and other federal installations.

Political necessity is the prime mover in Washington. By necessity, the White House staff finds it must respond to members of Congress; a telephone call by an important member to the White House congressional-liaison staff can sometimes make things move. The White House staff can also, at times, be the final arbiter in disputes between the private sector and the executive departments and agencies. Its power is illusory; it rests largely on the talents and personalities of its staff.

The staff is the source for all presidential letters and messages.

Whenever you request a presidential message, inform the White House staff as to the purpose of the message; the details you want included in it; to whom it should be addressed; and the date by which it is needed. Provide the staff with as much information (brochures, publications) as possible about yourself or your group; you may also want to provide it with a draft of the message. In addition, requests for messages should be placed at least six months in advance. Limit your dealings to one staff person, be courteous, and do not hesitate to inform the staff of the political value of the message for the President. If necessary, explain how that constituency can prove of value to the President.

It is always a good idea to develop contacts with the White House staff; do not discount the value of the lower echelons of the staff. A soldier can sometimes prove more valuable to you than a general; the former can tell you how things get done and will sometimes help you get them done.

Agencies that Make Policy

Within the Executive Office are also found a number of important policy-making agencies; these little-known governmental bodies can impact profoundly on our daily lives. Some of these agencies are advisory bodies to the President; they are his messengers to the bureaucracy and the Congress. They coordinate presidential programs and policies. They are open to public input and can provide you with an alternative arena should you reach an impasse with the federal bureaucracy.

Office of Management and Budget (OMB)

Established pursuant to the Reorganization Plan of 1970, OMB is headed by a director who is selected by the President. The Director of OMB can prove to be a significant figure in the Executive Office; however, much of this will depend on his personality and that of the President. Because of its broad powers, OMB exerts great influence over the federal government. Among other things, OMB:

Assists the President in reviewing the organizational structure and management procedures of the executive branch of government.

Develops efficient mechanisms for the implementation of government programs and activities.

Assists the President in the preparation of the budget and the formulation of the fiscal program.

Coordinates and clears departmental recommendations and proposed legislation, and makes recommendations to the President as regards future legislation.

Assists in the preparation of proposed executive orders and proclamations.

Assists the President in the assessment of program objectives.

Keeps the President informed on the progress of government agency activities.

OMB is also responsible for ensuring that the moneys appropriated by Congress for running the federal government are expended in the most economical manner. The agency reviews questionnaires that government agencies wish to send to the private sector, and decides whether these are burdensome or a duplication of information readily available through other channels.

A key component of OMB is its Office of Regulatory and Information Policy (ORIP). The primary responsibility of ORIP is to develop and supervise regulatory reform programs; ORIP also seeks to encourage and expand interagency coordination. It is responsible for reducing unnecessary paperwork and excessive red tape in the federal bureaucracy.

OMB compiles a number of important reports on the bureaucracy for the President. Many of these reports are public and readily available by writing to: Office of the Director, Office of Management and Budget, Executive Office Building, Washington, D.C. 20503.

National Security Council (NSC)

Established in 1947 by the National Security Act,[3] NSC is chaired by the President and the Vice-President; the Secretaries of State and Defense are its other key members. The Chairman of the Joint Chiefs of Staff acts as its military adviser, while the Director of the CIA acts as its intelligence adviser. NSC advises the President on all matters dealing with or affecting national security.

One of the key components of NSC is the CIA. The CIA is primarily responsible for the following.[4]

Collection of foreign intelligence

Coordination of foreign-intelligence efforts with the FBI

Collection, production, and dissemination of intelligence on foreign aspects of narcotics production and trafficking

Activities of foreign counterintelligence

Production and dissemination of counterintelligence studies and reports

Research and development of matters relating to national security

The CIA, however, is not a domestic police agency. It does not have domestic surveillance, investigatory, or subpoena powers; nor does it play a direct internal security function. These powers are allocated to other agencies. It is an important component of NSC and plays a key role in the development of foreign policy.

Office of the Special Representative for Trade Negotiations

Established under the Trade Act of 1974, the office carries out its mandate under the authority of the Trade Expansion Act of 1962.[5] The office is headed by a Special Representative for Trade Negotiations, who holds a cabinet-level title and the rank of ambassador. The representative is directly responsible to the President and is often a staunch party loyalist; the job has usually gone to a high party official. The representative directs trade negotiations with foreign nations, and is responsible for supervising and coordinating present trade agreements.

Domestic Policy Staff (DPS)

Established in 1977 under Reorganization Plan No. 1, the mission of the DPS is to formulate and coordinate domestic-policy recommendations to the President.[6] The DPS also assesses national needs and priorities, and advises the President on domestic issues. It maintains and provides a continuous review of ongoing programs from a domestic-policy standpoint.

The Executive Office is a conglomoration of diverse agencies; the ones discussed in this chapter are only a portion. These have diverse jurisdictions and interests; the interests of their constituencies also vary. They advise and consult with the President, and constitute the bureaucracy of the Executive Office. Their power and input on decision making will depend in large part on the people who head and staff these agencies, and also on the personality and interests of the President. Like the rest of the federal bureaucracy, these agencies are open to input from the public.

Notes

1. Article II, sec. 1.
2. 5 U.S.C. 133–133r and 133t.
3. See, 50 U.S.C. 402.
4. See, 50 U.S.C. 402 et seq.
5. See, 19 U.S.C. 2171.
6. See, 19 U.S.C. 1801.

9

Policing Wall Street Is the SEC's Job

A federal court finds a national law firm liable for more than $20 million in damages, for alleged violations of the federal securities laws by several of its lawyers. A stockbroker with a small midwestern firm is suspended from doing business for a period of two years. The chief executive of a California-based manufacturing firm is subpoenaed by investigators for the Securities and Exchange Commission (SEC). These are but a few cases involving the SEC—the agency that polices Wall Street.

Businesspeople, lawyers, professionals both within and outside the securities industry, and the public in general have a stake in how the SEC polices the nation's financial community. The survival of our economy depends in part on understanding how agencies like the SEC function.

How the Agency Functions

Like the other federal independent regulatory agencies, the SEC is bipartisan and vested with quasi-judicial functions. Congress has delegated to this agency the power to administer the nation's securities laws; the agency's primary objective is to protect the public's investments in the nation's securities industry. The SEC's powers rest on several key federal securities statutes, the most important of which are the Securities Act of 1933 and the Securities Exchange Act of 1934.[1]

Policymaking at the agency is formulated by a body of five commissioners, not more than three of whom may be members of the same party. The commissioners are appointed by the President, with the advice and consent of the Senate, for five-year terms; the chairman of the commission is designated by the President. The SEC is divided into five divisions and nine regional offices; investigations are conducted by its Enforcement Division. The agency's staff is made up of lawyers, accountants, securities analysts, and clerical employees.

Understanding the Federal Securities Laws

The objective of the national securities laws is twofold: to provide investors with accurate financial material and other pertinent data concerning the securities offered to the public for sale; and to prohibit misrepresentations, deceitful conduct, and other fraudulent acts and practices in the sale and purchase of securities. The securities laws apply to both domestic and private issuers, and cover the securities of foreign governments or their instrumentalities.

The agency's jurisdiction is far-reaching. The underlying objective of its enforcement program is to ensure that disclosures of financial material facts reported by publicly held corporations and others in the securities industry are both accurate and adequate. The securities laws prohibit the making of false and misleading statements, and the penalty for such acts consists of civil fines and criminal prosecution.

The federal securities laws also require that all national securities exchanges, broker–dealers, and other persons who conduct over-the-counter securities business in interstate or foreign commerce, be registered with the agency. In order to enforce the securities laws, the SEC is empowered to take any of the following measures.

Civil injunctive action

Criminal referrals to the U.S. Department of Justice for prosecution

Administrative sanctions

As regards civil injunctive action, the agency may apply to an appropriate federal district court for an order enjoining those acts and practices of an individual or corporation that is in violation of the securities laws. The SEC may also refer a case to the Department of Justice for criminal prosecution. The agency itself has no criminal statutory jurisdiction.

The agency may take internal administrative action against an individual or corporation. This can result in the suspension or expulsion of that individual or corporation from the exchanges or from the over-the-counter dealers associations. The agency may deny, suspend, or revoke the registration of a stockbroker. All SEC administrative actions are heard by an administrative law judge or hearing examiner. In these hearings, the agency wears two hats—it acts both as prosecutor and judge. An aggrieved party, however, has the right to appeal all of the agency's decisions to a U.S. court of appeals.

Disclosure and Registration Requirements

The federal securities laws require that all issuers of securities who make public offerings first file a registration statement with the SEC.[2] However, government securities, nonpublic offerings, intrastate offerings, and offerings not in excess of $500,000 are exempt from these registration requirements. If a registration statement is found to contain material misstatements or omissions, it can be refused or suspended. The agency may bar the sale of the securities until the statement is amended; however, the agency must accord the party an opportunity to present rebuttal evidence.

The securities laws require that all national securities exchanges and associations register with the SEC. In addition, any corporation whose securities are listed with the exchanges and which has asets of $1 million and/or 500 or more shareholders of record, must file periodic reports with the agency. Officers, directors, and large stockholders are likewise required to file detailed information with the SEC as regards their holdings and financial transactions.

Fraud in the purchase or sale of securities will often result in an SEC enforcement action. Broker–dealers and investment advisers who willfully violate the securities laws or any of the SEC rules and regulations run the risk of being the targets of an investigation. If they are found to have violated the securities laws, they can be suspended or expelled from the national securities exchanges or the National Association of Securities Dealers. Although the agency has authority to refer criminal infractions to the Justice Department, it rarely does so. The threat of such action, however, sometimes suffices to induce a witness to cooperate.

Expulsions, although few and far between, do occur. Attorneys, accountants, and other securities professionals who are found to be in violation of the securities laws face the loss of their privilege to practice before the agency. Since practicing before the SEC can often be financially rewarding, expulsion can prove devastating. Such action may also make the professional a target of lawsuits by other parties, as well as bring about the possible loss of his privilege to practice before the other federal agencies. It should be pointed out, however, that the SEC is often reluctant to resort to such action.

How the Rules of Practice Operate

If you must deal with the SEC, you can represent yourself, your partnership, or your corporation. You may also appear on behalf of a state commission or political division. It is not necessary to be represented by an attorney when dealing with the agency.

However, it is advisable that you employ counsel in complex cases. The counsel must be admitted to practice before the U.S. Supreme Court or the highest court of the state or territory in which he practices. When

appearing before the SEC, an individual or his counsel should inform
the agency in writing of his appearance and the purpose of his appearance. He should also list his address and telephone number.

The right to appear or practice before the agency is a privilege which
the agency can either revoke or temporarily suspend. There are a number
of reasons why the SEC can revoke or suspend the right of an individual.
These can involve one or more of the following.

The individual does not possess the requisite qualifications to represent himself or others before the agency.

The individual is lacking in character or integrity, or has/is engaged
in unethical or improper professional conduct.

The individual has willfully violated or aided others to violate the
provisions of the securities laws.

The individual has been convicted of a crime in state or federal court.

The individual has been disciplined, barred, or suspended from practicing before another federal agency.

However, keep in mind that although the agency manages to make
the financial section of the *New York Times* and the *Washington Post,*
few in the Washington legal community view the SEC with trepidation.
It barks more times than it bites. Few dishonest professionals have been
permanently barred from practicing before the SEC. Often suspension
consists of a slap on the wrist; for example, one attorney who was suspended for three months managed to work it out so that the suspension
coincided with his vacation to Europe. Suspension and revocation are
viewed as extreme positions by the agency; to be barred one has to border
on criminal activity.

When faced with suspension, an individual has several options open
to him. Within three days after being notified of the SEC's suspension
order, one can petition the agency to lift it. After the SEC receives his
petition, it must decide to either lift the suspension order or have the
case scheduled for a hearing. At which time, the individual can present
evidence and witnesses in support of his petition. This also serves to bog
down the agency for several months. Should he fail to petition the agency,
the suspension order will become final thirty days from the date he
received it.

SEC suspension hearings involving professionals are known as Rule
2(e) Hearings. They are often nonpublic, unless the agency decides on
its own motion or the motion of a third party to make them public. The
subject of a proceeding, however, stands to gain little by requesting the

SEC to make the hearing public. A public hearing could subject him to ridicule and civil action.

How Enforcement Actions Work

The SEC's investigative responsibilities are handled by both its Washington-based Enforcement Division and the staffs of its regional offices. SEC investigations are private and confidential; the evidence gathered in the course of an investigation is deemed to be nonpublic, unless its commission deems otherwise. A witness or target of an SEC investigation who submits original documents with the staff is entitled to copies of these; in addition, any person who gives testimony is also entitled to a transcript of his testimony. The SEC staff will often refuse to provide transcripts of other witnesses' testimony while the investigation is still open. The agency, however, will charge a fee for the preparation of a transcript.

The agency is empowered to authorize its staff to conduct a formal investigation whenever it has reasonable basis to believe that an individual or corporation has or is about to violate the federal securities laws, or any of the agency's rules and regulations. However, *reasonableness* can be interpreted broadly and narrowly; this will depend on the political views of the agency's commission.

All SEC investigations commence as informal inquiries. They often take the form of an informal telephone call or letter from the agency's staff to a potential witness or target. These inquiries are often the result of a complaint or tip from someone in the securities industry. They take the form of a fishing expedition; the staff is merely checking out the complaint or tip. If it finds that there is reasonable basis to pursue the matter further, it will then press ahead for tangible evidence to convince its superiors to authorize a formal investigation.

Once the staff has sufficient evidence to convince the commission that infractions have or are about to take place, it will request from the commission a formal order of investigation. When requesting such an order, the staff will prepare a memorandum addressed to the commission which details the potential violations and potential targets. The formal order will empower it to issue subpoenas, take testimony, and obtain other evidence. The staff is not required to notify an individual or corporation that it is the subject of its investigation.

A copy of a formal order may be provided if one writes to the Director of the Enforcement Division. Although the director has broad discretion and can refuse a request (especially if his investigators are opposed to the disclosure), approval is the norm. A copy of the order will be supplied at no cost. Whether compelled to appear or appearing voluntarily, a witness has the right to be accompanied by counsel of his choosing. Indigents may request a local public defender's office to represent them; however, since all SEC investigations are civil in nature, the agency does not feel compelled to provide counsel nor pay counsel fees.

Witnesses in SEC investigations are interviewed privately. Only their attorneys of record may accompany them and be present during the interview. Counsel for a witness can advise his client before, during, and after the interview, and take notes during the examination for his use only. If a witness or his attorney should engage in obstructionist tactics during the course of the interview or the investigation, the staff is authorized to take all requisite steps to safeguard the integrity of the process. It may bar the obstructionist attorney from accompanying his client to any other proceedings. However, the agency will often take no action; it will avoid any actions that can spark publicity.

Witnesses can assert their constitutional right against self-incrimination at any stage of the investigation. The SEC staff has no power to grant witnesses immunity from criminal prosecution. It can, however, recommend to its commission that it place such a request with the Justice Department. It is important to remember that the SEC itself has no authority to grant any form of immunity from prosecution.[3]

Many of the SEC's investigations deal with the manipulation of the market price of securities; misappropriation or unlawful hypothecation of a customer's funds or securities; insider trading; and purchases or sale of securities by a broker–dealer at prices not reasonably related to the current market price. Payoff and kickback schemes by corporations have also been the targets of SEC investigations. This is not to say, however, that the agency has contained the problem of fraud in Wall Street; rather, the overwhelming majority of these frauds are committed with impunity. Few are ever investigated and even fewer make their way to prosecution.

The likelihood of an SEC investigation resulting in a criminal prosecution is remote. The real threat to the culprits stems from private sources—stockholder suits are common. Once an investigation is concluded, private parties can often gain access to the staff's investigatory files through an FOIA request. The evidence the staff has collected can prove valuable to private litigants. Thus, if you should be the victim of a securities fraud, the SEC's investigative files can be of value. Use the FOIA to gain access to its findings.

Targets and Their Representation

The majority of the witnesses in an SEC investigation are not the staff's targets; nor do the majority of the agency's investigations culminate in any enforcement action. However, to ensure that you are not abused by SEC investigators, it is best that you know your rights and also understand how the investigative process works. Remember that it is the task of the courts, and not the SEC investigators, to make a finding of guilt.

Whenever a witness is interviewed by the SEC staff in a formal investigation, a stenographic transcript is made of the testimony. Before you give any testimony, request that the SEC staff show you a copy of its formal order of investigation. If it fails to do so, inform them that you will not proceed any further until the order is shown. Once you see it, you can make a summary of its content.

After a witness has had an opportunity to review the order, the investigating officer will administer the oath and inform the witness of his Fifth Amendment right against self-incrimination. He is also told that any false (perjured) statements that he makes can be used to prosecute him under the U.S. Criminal Code.[4] The witness is then asked to produce any documents and other material that was subpoenaed by the staff.

Witnesses appearing pursuant to a subpoena are entitled to SEC witness and mileage fees. Counsel for the witness (or the witness himself) should request a reimbursement voucher from the staff. If a subpoena has been issued for the production of records, then the witness must either produce them or raise a constitutional objection. A witness who seeks to delay an investigation can do so by raising such an objection.

A witness will be asked numerous questions to determine how much knowledge he has of the events under investigation. Some of these questions will require the following information.

Any prior or present arrests, indictments, or convictions.

Any past or present civil or administrative actions brought against him.

Any prior testimony given before any court, governmental agency, or private regulatory group.

Whether the witness is registered with the SEC or any other government agency.

Any connections the witness may have with the other witnesses in the investigation.

A listing of any managerial or financial involvement (direct or indirect) in the events under investigation.

The locations of all securities and brokerage accounts in the witness's or his relatives' names, or any accounts over which he has a beneficial interest or discretionary control.

A listing of the names, locations, and addresses of all corporate or personal bank (checking and savings) accounts, loans and safe deposit boxes, either here or abroad.

The objectives of the SEC interview are to reconstruct the events under investigation, determine the role of the witness in these events, and ascertain if there were any violations of law (either by the witness or any other party).

Why the Agency Issues Subpoenas

The SEC staff can issue two types of subpoena: *subpoena ad testificandum* and *subpoena duces tecum*. The function of the former is to compel a witness to appear and give testimony; the function of the latter is to compel the witness to produce documents, as well as give testimony. If a witness is asked to provide documents in response to a subpoena, he should always provide photocopies; never provide the originals. The staff, however, may want to see the originals at the time of the interview.

Although the courts frown on the use of administrative subpoenas for purposes of gathering evidence for criminal prosecution, it is not unusual for the staff of the SEC or any other agency to do so. If the staff is found to employ its subpoenas to assist investigators or prosecutors in other civil or criminal cases, objections can be made to its commission.

The agency's subpoenas, like those of other regulatory bodies, are administrative in nature. To enforce them, the SEC's staff must both inform its commission that the witness has failed to comply with their subpoena, and request that the commission authorize it to go to federal court for the purpose of enforcing it. The commission, however, is often reluctant to authorize such action; even if it does, the investigation may be delayed for several months because of the commission's backlog. Subpoena enforcement actions can be time-consuming, and are rarely authorized unless the target of the investigation is a real bad apple.

If a witness wants to challenge the staff's subpoena, he can do so by filing a motion in opposition to it with the commission. If this happens, then the staff must file a reply to the motion. The staff may modify the subpoena or, in an effort not to make waves in the agency, drop the subpoena altogether. However, the commission (if it supports the staff's efforts) may let it go to court and seek enforcement. Regardless of the outcome, the witness has bought valuable time by filing an opposition motion to the staff's subpoena. The witness has also ensured that he will not be held in contempt for failure to comply, should the staff's enforcement action find favor with the court.

Much has been said and written about the SEC. Its supporters portray it as a supercop keeping Wall Street straight. To its opponents, it has come to symbolize regulation at its worst. It is neither. Simply put, it has traditionally been one of Washington's more aggressive regulatory agencies. In dealing with the SEC, you do not need the services of overpriced lobbyists and lawyers; you simply need to understand its modus operandi and how it fits into the federal bureaucratic maze. Armed with this knowledge, you may be able to employ it to your advantage.

Notes

1. See, 15 U.S.C. 77a et seq.; and 78a–78jj.
2. See, 15 U.S.C. 77a et seq.
3. For a detailed discussion of the use of immunity, see the Organized Crime Control Act of 1970 (18 U.S.C. 600 et seq.).
4. Even if a witness is not administered an oath, he can still be prosecuted under 18 U.S.C. 1001 for making false statements. In practice, however, few SEC witnesses have ever been prosecuted for perjury.

Appendix 9A
Handling Securities-
Related Disputes

Small investors inundate government agencies with complaints against their stockholders. There are a number of inexpensive routes open to you for settling small disputes. You can always file a formal complaint with the Securities and Exchange Commission or a state agency. In addition, you can also submit your complaint to formal arbitration, but use the courts only as a last resort. The decision of the arbitration is considered final. Complaints can be filed with one or more of the following

Securities and Exchange Commission
Complaint Section
500 North Capitol St.
Washington, D.C. 20549

National Association of Securities Dealers
1735 K St., N.W.
Washington, D.C. 20006

Securities Investor Protection Corp.
900 17th St., N.W.
Washington, D.C. 20006

American Stock Exchange
Department of Inquiries
85 Trinity Place
New York, NY 10006

The New York Stock Exchange Investor Service Bureau
11 Wall St.
New York, NY 10006

Appendix 9B
Sample Charges in Federal Securities Prosecutions

A. Violations under the Securities Act of 1933
   1. Unregistered securities—Sec. 5(a) & (C)
   2. Insufficient and inadequate prospectus—Sec. 5(b)
B. Violations under the Securities Exchange Act of 1934
   1. Margin, credit, Regulation T
      a. Member firms—Sec. 7(c)(1)
      b. General account—withdrawals below minimum margin requirements—Sec. 7(c)(1)
      c. Special accounts—improper handling—Sec. 7(c)(1)
   2. Commingling securities without consent—Sec. 8(c)–1(a)
   3. Price manipulation—Sec. 9
   4. Failure to mark orders *long* or *short*—Sec. 10(a) and Rule 10a–1
   5. Broker–dealer unregistered—Sec. 15(a):
      a. Transacting business
      b. Aiding and abetting unregistered broker–dealer
   6. Broker-dealer applications—Sec. 15(b):
      a. Application inaccurate—Rule 15(b)(1)1
      b. False financial information reported—Rule 15(b)(1)2
      c. Failure promptly to amend—Rule 15(b)(3)1
      d. Amendment inaccurate—Rule 15(b)(3)1
      e. Withdrawal application false—Rule 15(b)(6)1
   7. Books and records, Broker–dealer—Sec. 17(a):
      a. False entries—Rule 17a–3
      b. Failure to maintain accurately—Rule 17a–3
      c. Failure to preserve—Rule 17a–4
      d. Failure to file report of financial condition—Rule 17a–5
      e. False reporting of financial condition—Rule 17a–5

Appendix 9C
Sample SEC
Documents

CERTIFIED MAIL
RETURN RECEIPT REQUESTED

In the Matter of:

TO: (Name and address of respondent)

Please find enclosed an order for proceedings pursuant to Section 15 of the Securities Exchange Act of 1934 in the above-captioned matter.

Your particular attention is directed to Section IV of the order which requires you to file an answer pursuant to Rule 7 of the Commission's Rules of Practice (17 CFR 201.7). Rules 6 and 7 of the Commission's Rules of Practice (17 CFR 201.6 and 201.7) provide that if you fail to file the required answer or fail to appear at a hearing after being duly notified, you shall be deemed in default and the proceedings may be determined against you upon consideration of the order for proceedings, the allegations of which will be deemed to be true. In this connection, please be aware that when a registrant is found to be in default, it is the Commission's policy to enter an order pursuant to Section 15(b)(7) of the Securities Exchange Act of 1934 barring such individual from becoming associated with a broker or dealer.

If you have any questions or wish to discuss any aspect of the proceedings, you may communicate with the (name of) Regional Office, (address of office).

Very truly yours,

Secretary

Figure 9C–1. Sample Notice of Order for Proceedings

UNITED STATES OF AMERICA
before
SECURITIES AND EXCHANGE COMMISSION

SECURITIES EXCHANGE ACT OF 1934
Rel. No.

Admin. Proc. File No.

In the Matter of

(name and address of
respondent)

FINDINGS AND ORDER IMPOSING REMEDIAL SANCTION

In these broker–dealer proceedings under the Securities Exchange Act, (name of respondent), a salesman for a registered broker–dealer, has submitted an offer of settlement which the Commission has determined to accept. Solely for the purpose of this proceeding and any other proceeding brought by the Commission, and without admitting or denying the allegations in the order for proceeding brought by the Commission, and without admitting or denying the allegations in the order for proceedings, respondent consents to findings of misconduct as alleged in that order and to the imposition of a specified sanction.

On the basis of the order for proceedings and the offer of settlement, it is found that, during the period from about (fill date) to (fill date), Section 10(b) of the Exchange Act and Rule 10b–5 thereunder in that, in the offer and sale of common stock of XYZ Corporation, he made material misstatements and omissions with respect to the company's financial condition and substantial operating losses; its present and prospective government contracts; its growth potential as compared with that of established, highly successful companies; the speculative nature of an investment in the stock; prospective increases in its market price; the purchase of the stock by (name of respondent) for investment; mutual funds necessitating a hasty investment decision by the customer.

(continued)

Figure 9C–2. Sample Order Imposing Sanctions

Figure 9C–2 continued

In view of the foregoing, it is in the public interest to impose the sanction specified in the offer of settlement.

Accordingly, IT IS ORDERED that (name of respondent) and he hereby is, suspended from being associated with any broker or dealer for a period of _____ , effective as of the opening of business on (period order takes effect).

For the Commission by the Office of Opinions and Review, pursuant to delegated authority.

_____

Secretary (of Commission)

_____

ADMINISTRATIVE PROCEEDING
FILE NO.

U.S. SECURITIES AND EXCHANGE COMMISSION
Washington, D.C.

(NAME OF RESPONDENT) :	
:	REQUEST TO ENTER DEFAULT
(CASE NO.) :	

Respondent (name) in the above-captioned matter having failed to file an answer within the time prescribed by the Commission's Rules of Practice, the Division of (name of division) hereby requests that a default be entered with respect to said respondent that the Commission determine the proceedings pursuant to Rule 7 of the Commission's Rules of Practice.

Counsel for the Commission

Date _____

Figure 9C–3. Sample Administrative Trial Request to Enter Default

U.S. SECURITIES AND EXCHANGE COMMISSION
Washington, D.C.

_____

(NAME OF RESPONDENT) :

                           : ADMINISTRATIVE PROCEEDING

(CASE NO.)   : FILE NO.

                           :

_____:

CERTIFICATE OF SERVICE

I hereby certify that on the _____day of _____ ,
19_____ , I caused to be served by United States certified airmail
true copies of the Request to Enter Default upon the person(s) whose
name(s) and address(es) is herewith set forth:

(NAME AND ADDRESS OF PERSON OR PERSONS SERVED)

_____

          Counsel for the Commission

Date_____

Figure 9C–4. Sample Administrative Trial Certificate of Service on
         Default Request

UNITED STATES DISTRICT COURT
FOR THE DISTRICT OF COLUMBIA

SECURITIES AND EXCHANGE COMMISSION,
          Plaintiff
 	
     v.
 	
(NAME OF DEFENDANT),
 	
         Defendant
	)
	)
	)
	) CIVIL ACTION
	) NO.
	)
	)
	) STIPULATION AND CONSENT
	) OF (NAME OF DEFENDANT)
	)

Defendant (NAME) hereby consents and agrees as follows:

I

Defendant, for purposes of this action only and the enforcement of this Judgment, enters a general appearance, acknowledges receipt of the Complaint filed herein and admits the jurisdiction of this Court over him and over the subject matter of this action.

II

Defendant consents that this Court, forthwith and without further notice may enter the annexed Final Judgment of Permanent Injunction and Ancillary Relief ("Judgment").

III

Defendant, in consenting to the entry of the annexed Judgment, does so without admitting or denying any of the allegations made by the plaintiff Securities and Exchange Commission ("Commission") in its Complaint herein.

IV

The Commission and the defendant waive entry of findings of fact and conclusions of law under Rule 52 of the Federal Rules of Civil Procedure.

(continued)

Figure 9C–5. Sample Consent Order

Figure 9C–5 continued

V

Defendant agrees that this Court shall retain jurisdiction over him upon entry of the Judgment annexed hereto for the purpose of enforcing or modifying such Final Judgment.

VI

Defendant states that he enters into this Consent voluntarily, and that no promise, threat or representation of any kind has been made by the Commission or by any member, officer, agent, employee or representative thereof to induce him to enter into this Consent.

VII

The Commission states that nothing in the annexed Judgment, this Consent, or any other Consent entered in connection with the annexed Judgment shall be deemed a determination by the Commission that the amount of payments referred to in Paragraph VI of the annexed Judgment is the full amount owed to XYZ Corporation or any other corporation by the defendant on account of the matters alleged in the Complaint or similar matters.

VIII

Defendant agrees that, in all elections of directors of public related companies (as such term is defined in the annexed Judgment) held during the period of time during which the provisions of Paragraph VII of the annexed Judgment are in effect as to such companies, he will vote or cause to be voted all shares under his direct or indirect control in favor of management's candidates for the independent directorships referred to in Paragraph VII of the annexed Judgment, and will do nothing to interfere with the nomination or election of such independent directors.

STIPULATED TO:

BY: _____

(DEFENDANT)

Date:

BY: _____

(NAME OF GOVERNMENT
ATTORNEY)

Date:

Securities Act Release No.   Administrative Proceeding File No.

UNITED STATES OF AMERICA
before the
SECURITIES AND EXCHANGE COMMISSION

In the Matter of	: ORDER INSTITUTING
	: PROCEEDINGS
(name of respondent)	: AND IMPOSING SANCTIONS
	: PURSUANT
(address)	: TO RULE 2(e) OF THE
	: COMMISSION'S
	: RULES OF PRACTICE
Rules of Practice	:
Rule 2(e)	:
	:
	:

The Commission deems it appropriate that proceedings be instituted against (name of respondent), pursuant to Rule 2(e) of the Commission's Rules of Practice with respect to his qualifications to appear and practice before the Commission. Accordingly, IT IS ORDERED that such proceedings be, and they hereby are, instituted.

(Name of respondent) has submitted an offer of settlement for the purpose of disposing of issues raised in these proceedings. Under the terms of his offer of settlement, (name of respondent), solely for purposes of these proceedings and without admitting or denying the factual assertions set forth herein, consents to findings against him as set forth hereafter and to imposition by the Commission of censure.

1. The respondent (name) is a practicing attorney at law with offices in (city and state).
2. (summary of facts which led to censure)
3. (description of the respondent and his role).
4. (summary of violations).

(continued)

Figure 9C–6. Sample Order Instituting 2(e) Proceedings

Figure 9C–6 continued

5. Respondent thereby wilfully aided and abetted violations of Section _____ of the Securities Act of 1933, 15 U.S.C., and Section _____ of the Securities Exchange Act of 1934, 15 U.S.C., and Rule _____ thereunder, 17 CFR _____ .

After due consideration, and upon the recommendation of the staff, the Commission has determined to accept respondents offer of consent to a censure in the Rule 2(e) proceeding herein. In arriving at its determination that the only sanction be a censure, the Commission has taken into consideration the fact that respondent and the firm in which he is a partner have adopted procedures designed to insure against a recurrence of the aforementioned volative activities and to take all reasonable steps to conduct his professional practice in accordance with such procedures. Further, the Commission notes that neither respondent nor his law firm has ever before been a respondent in an administrative proceeding instituted pursuant to Rule 2(e) of the Commission's Rules of Practice or a defendant in an injunctive action brought by the Commission.

Accordingly, IT IS ORDERED, pursuant to Rule 2(e) of the Commission's Rules of Practice, and subject to the terms and conditions set forth above, the respondent be, and hereby is, censured by the Commission.

By the Commission.

_____

Secretary (of Commission)

UNITED STATES OF AMERICA
Before the
SECURITIES AND EXCHANGE COMMISSION

SECURITIES ACT OF 1933
Rel. No.: _____
Admin. Proc. File No.: _____

In the Matter   )
)
(Name and address of   )
Respondent)   )
Rule 2(e), Rules of Practice   )

The Commission having issued an order pursuant to Rule 2(e)(3)(i)(A) of its Rules of Practice temporarily suspending (name of Respondent), an attorney, from appearing or practicing before it;

Respondent having sought review of the aforementioned temporary suspension order in the United States Court of Appeals for the District of Columbia Circuit;

That court having dismissed respondent's petition for review without opinion;

Respondent having thereafter filed a petition with the Commission for an order lifting the temporary suspension;

The Commission having denied said petition and having set the matter down for hearing before an administrative law judge to determine what permanent sanction, if any, should be imposed on respondent;

Such evidentiary hearing having been waived by the parties, and an initial decision by the administrative law judge also having been waived;

The record having been stipulated;

Briefs having been filed, and oral argument having been heard;

(continued)

Figure 9C–7. Sample Order Permanently Denying Privilege of Practice

Figure 9C–7 continued

The Commission having this day issued its Findings and Opinion, on the basis of said Findings and Opinion, it is pursuant to Rule 2(e)(3)(iii) of the Commission's Rules of Practice ORDERED that <u>(name of Respondent)</u> be, and he hereby is, permanently disqualified from appearing or practicing before the Commission.

By the Commission.

_____

Secretary (of Commission)

10 The USDA Does More than Inspect

A ham maker wants to label his product "Country Ham"; he applies to the U.S. Department of Agriculture (USDA) for approval, but is stopped in his tracks. The USDA staff tells him that the label can only be carried by those pork products that fall within the department's definition of *country*. In another instance, a rancher who wants to expand his ranching operations receives a guaranteed loan from one of the USDA's agencies.

Each year the department reviews more than 200,000 applications from individuals and companies seeking approval of new labels for meat products, and loans and grants. The department does more than regulate the sale of farm-related commodities, it also guarantees loans, provides technical assistance, and funds numerous agricultural-related programs. With offices both within and outside this country, the USDA is an important source of information and funds.

Structure and Organization

The USDA was created by an act of Congress and many of the federal agricultural programs were placed under the USDA's direct jurisdiction.[1] The department also assumes control over many of Washington's agricultural assistance programs; these run in the billions of dollars annually. Its programs reach into both rural and urban America; the former is not its only constituency.

The Secretary of Agriculture is the principal officer of the department; his key adviser is the Assistant Secretary for Administration. It is the latter who is responsible for USDA administrative matters. Another important USDA official is the General Counsel; he is the secretary's legal adviser, and all legal matters that relate to USDA are reviewed and often handled by his staff. Criminal and civil USDA-related prosecutions, however, are the province of the Department of Justice (DOJ).

With the growth of USDA programs since World War II, departmental programs have been plagued by fraud, waste, and abuse. Thus, the department's Inspector General has in the last several years assumed the role of auditor and policeman; his staff investigates all allegations of fraud and waste, and refers criminal cases to the DOJ for action. The

133

staff also investigates allegations of conflict of interest or unethical conduct involving USDA employees.

There are a number of other agencies and offices that play an important role in the USDA. Among these are the Farmers Home Administration (FmHA) and the Rural Electrification Administration (REA). Knowing how these function and their jurisdictions could prove of value to any person or company that is engaged in or has dealings with the agricultural sector. Knowing which agency or office to contact with a problem can save you time and money.

The Dealings of the FmHA

The role of the Farmers Home Administration (FmHA) is to provide credit and assistance to individuals and businesses that (for whatever reason) are unable to obtain credit elsewhere.[2] Applications for FmHA loans can be made at any of its local offices; the FmHA loans are attractive because of their favorable rates and terms. However, before the agency will extend a loan, an applicant must first be certified as being qualified by a three-member committee; at least two of the committee members are farmers.

There is a variety of FmHA loans for which an applicant may qualify; the only requirement is that the money be used for a farm-related project. Among the available programs, are the following.

1. Operating Loans. These are targeted for the small farmer who cannot obtain credit from a private source. To qualify for a loan, the borrower must employ the funds to improve the use of his land. Under this broad definition, even recreational enterprises have been known to qualify. However, the loans are more commonly made for such things as farm equipment, seed, livestock, and other farm-related needs. The interest rate charged is fixed yearly by the Secretary of Agriculture; the borrower has up to seven years to repay the loan.

2. Youth Project Loans. Residents of rural communities who are under twenty-one years of age can qualify for these loans. Their purpose is to assist the borrower in producing income from farm-related enterprises. The interest rate on the loan is determined annually, and is often attractive.

3. Emergency Loans. These loans are available to farmers and ranchers who have suffered any loss or operating costs as a result of some natural disaster.

4. Emergency Livestock Loan Guarantees. Ranchers and farmers

who are faced with adverse economic conditions can apply for these FmHA guaranteed loans. The loan itself is made by a legal lender, and must be repaid within seven years; however, it can be renewed for an additional three years.

5. Farm Ownership Loans. These are available to farmers and ranchers who are in need of funds to buy additional agricultural land; however, only family-size operations can qualify. These loans are also available for the purpose of constructing or repairing farm buildings and for general land and water improvements; they are made at low interest rates, and must be repaid within forty years.

6. Soil and Conservation Loans. Private persons and corporations can qualify for this program. The purpose is to assist the farmer in improving the condition of his land; however, the applicant must first demonstrate that the improvements are conservation related. The loan must be repaid within forty years.

7. Recreational Loans. These loans are available to farmers for the purpose of converting their land into income-producing recreational enterprises.

8. Loans to Indian Tribes. These are available only to select Indian tribes and tribal corporations, for the purpose of enabling them to purchase lands within the tribal reservation. These low-interest loans must be repaid within forty years.

9. Rural Housing Loans. These are specifically targeted for small rural communities; the funds, however, must be used solely to purchase, construct, or repair essential farm buildings. Both poor and affluent farmers alike can qualify; builders, nonprofit corporations, consumer cooperatives, state and local agencies, and other profit and nonprofit organizations have also been held to qualify. The loan must be repaid within forty years.

10. Resource Conservation and Development Loans. An applicant for this loan must first be approved by the Soil Conservation Service, and the money must be used solely for conservation-connected programs. The loan must be repaid within fifty years.

11. Community Facility Loans. These are targeted for public and quasi-public agencies, nonprofit organizations, and specific Indian tribes. The applicant must first demonstrate that the purpose of the loan is to develop or safeguard water and waste-disposal systems.

12. Rural Industrialization Loans. These loans are available to both profit and nonprofit, public and private organizations; as well as to specific Indian tribes. Their purpose is to stimulate growth in rural communities with populations of under 50,000.

13. Watershed Protection and Flood Prevention Loans. Only local groups that have first been approved by the Soil Conservation Service can qualify for these. The money must be used solely to finance projects that serve to protect or develop land and water resources, and small watersheds. The loan must be repaid within fifty years.

Any individual, partnership, organization, or corporation (profit or nonprofit) engaged in any agricultural-connected activity can potentially qualify for one of these FmHA loans. Profit-making groups are not excluded, and financial need is not the determining factor. The programs are open to all members of the public. For an update on these programs, contact FmHA's Information Staff in Washington.

What the Agricultural Marketing Service (AMS) Does

Like some of the other USDA agencies, the AMS can be a valuable resource tool to those individuals, companies, and organizations that are involved in agricultural work. The AMS offers numerous services and also financial assistance to those who are versed in its operations. The agency provides the following.

Marketing information dealing with such things as supply, demand, prices, management, and location of agricultural products

Inspection, grading, and classifying services (for a small fee) for the buyers and sellers of such commodities as cotton, tobacco, wool, and mohair

Regulatory programs to safeguard producers and handlers from fraudulent practices[3]

Marketing agreements and orders to establish minimum prices for such commodities as fruits, vegetables, and milk[4]

Plant protection programs for developers of novel or unique varieties of plants, granting them exclusive rights to sell, reproduce, import, or export these plants

Funds for research and promotion

Other Marketing Services such as financial assistance for state-connected agricultural projects and promotional assistance for producers[5]

The Commodity Credit Corporation (CCC)

The CCC was created under Executive Order No. 6340 as a corporation of the federal government, and incorporated in Delaware. The corporation has a board of directors that is subject to the supervision of the USDA Secretary. It is authorized to administer loan and purchase-payment programs for such commodities as tobacco, wool, honey, wheat, corn, peanuts, and milk.

The CCC also has authority to sell surplus agricultural products to foreign governments. In addition, it administers such legislative programs as the:

Food and Agricultural Act of 1977, which authorizes the CCC to make disaster payments to producers of feed grains, wheat, and cotton or financial losses they have suffered as a result of some natural disaster or economic condition beyond their control; and

Agriculture and Development Trade Assistance Act of 1954, which authorizes the CCC to make loans to producers for the construction of facilities for the storage of grains, rice, soy beans, peanuts, dry beans, and sunflower seeds.

The Federal Crop Insurance Corporation (FCIC)

The FCIC is a corporate entity which is owned and administered by the federal government. Management of the corporation rests with a board of directors which falls under the supervision of the USDA Secretary. The FCIC is authorized to provide farmers with insurance coverage against financial losses caused by a natural disaster.

The FCIC's insurance program is available (for a small premium) for a variety of fruit, grain, and vegetable crops, as well as for cotton and tobacco. The administrative costs of these programs are funded annually by the Congress. The crop insurance program, however, will not cover any financial loss which is the outcome of neglect or poor farming practices.

Agriculture Stabilization and Conservation Service (ASCS)

The ASCS is one of the newer USDA agencies; it was established for the purpose of administering farm-connected stabilization programs for such commodities as wheat, corn, cotton, and honey. The agency carries this out through loans, purchases, and direct payments to producers; for example, the ASCS purchases surplus milk from producers. It also administers assistance programs to tobacco, peanut, and cotton growers.

The ASCS indemnifies beekeepers for the loss of any of their honey bees; it also provides financial assistance to owners of livestock for up to 50 percent of the cost of feed they have lost as the result of any natural disasters. In addition, the agency administers disaster payments to wheat, feed grain, and cotton farmers. For additional information, contact the agency's Information Division, Washington, D.C.

Rural Electrification Administration (REA)

The REA administers relief programs to help finance electric and telephone services in rural communities; it is one of the New Deal agencies. The agency's statutory authority rests on the Rural Electrification Act of 1936;[6] it serves primarily as a lending institution. The REA is authorized to make low-interest loans from the Electrification and Telephone Revolving Fund of the United States Treasury.

The REA is also authorized to guarantee loans made by private institutions; the borrower, however, is required to finance a part of the project from non-REA sources. The agency is under a congressional mandate to give first preference to nonprofit groups, cooperative associations, and public institutions. Some two-thirds of all REA-financed programs are to commercial companies; the remaining one-third are to subscriber-owned cooperatives.

Federal Grain Inspection Service (FGIS)

The FGIS was established in 1976 as an agency of the USDA; its primary responsibility is to carry out the provisions of the Grain Standards Act.[7] The agency is responsible for establishing national grain-inspection standards. It requires large grain exporters to register with it, and also supervises the inspection of all grain loaded on vessels for export. If a buyer or seller is not satisfied with the results of the FGIS inspection, he can appeal it to the local FGIS field office.

If not satisfied with the decision of the field office, he can then appeal the decision to the U.S. Board of Appeals and Review. The board is headquartered in Washington, and has authority to overturn a field-office decision. FGIS inspection standards are published in the Federal Register, and cover corn, wheat, rye, oats, barley, soy beans, and mixed grains. For additional information, contact the FGIS Information Division, Washington, D.C.

Other USDA Agencies

Many of the agency's executive departments are both regulators and resource tools. There are a number of agencies within the USDA that can be of assistance. For additional information on these, contact their individual information offices in Washington, D.C.

The *Animal and Plant Health Inspection Service (APHIS)* administers the USDA's pest and disease control and eradication programs. The agency is also authorized to regulate the importation of foreign plants, animals, and their products, and is responsible for the inspection and certification of domestic plants for export.

The *Food and Nutrition Service (FNS)* administers several important social programs.[8] Among these are the food-stamp program; child nutrition program; food distribution program; and supplemental food program.

The *Foreign Agricultural Service (FAS)* primarily functions to promote the export of American agricultural commodities. The agency also surveys foreign markets, and makes the information available to domestic exporters. It maintains offices in more than 100 countries; these can serve to address questions as regards specific countries.

The *Office of General Sales Manager (OGSM)* was established for the purpose of assisting exporters of agricultural products.[9] OGSM provides marketing and technical assistance, and it will also finance exports on a deferred-payment basis up to three years.

The *Science and Education Administration (SEA)* funds and coordinates agricultural research and training programs.[10] The SEA also provides technical assistance to farmers, producers, and handlers in such areas as soil conservation; use of organic waste material; plant and animal production; and the processing and distribution of agricultural products.

The *Soil Conservation Service (SCS)* is authorized by the Clean Water Act of 1977 to provide assistance to water improvement programs.[11] The SCS also carries out soil surveys, and funds local community watershed and flood-control programs.

The *Economics, Statistics, and Cooperative Services (ESCS)* conducts periodic surveys of consumer demands, pricing policies, and financial information for agricultural products. In addition, the ESCS publishes periodic reports on crops, fruits, vegetables, cattle, hogs, poultry, and other agricultural products. The agency also conducts special studies for agricultural cooperatives.

The USDA offers the following additional resources.

Reading rooms which are open to the public and are located at each of the regional offices

Training films (For information contact the USDA's Public Affairs Office in Washington)

Assorted publications dealing with numerous topics (available through the USDA Office of Governmental and Public Affairs in Washington)

A graduate school division which offers noncredit courses and is open to the public

Grants, loans, and programs (for additional information contact the USDA Office of Operations and Finance in Washington)

The USDA policies are geared to assist the agricultural constituencies; it is both a regulator and resource tool. It will investigate complaints and breaches of its rules and regulations; however, it is also a source of information, funds, and other assistance. Members of the public should learn to understand its operations and utilize its services; after all, the taxpayers fund its operations.

Notes

1. See, 5 U.S.C. 511–516.
2. See the *Code of Federal Regulations*. For a more detailed outline of FmHA jurisdiction and powers see 7 U.S.C. 1921.
3. See, 7 U.S.C. 181–229.
4. See, 7 U.S.C. 2321 et seq.
5. See, 7 U.S.C. 3001–3006.
6. See, 5 U.S.C. 301.
7. See, 7 U.S.C. 901–902.
8. See, 5 U.S.C. 301.
9. See, 5 U.S.C. 301.
10. See, 5 U.S.C. 301.
11. 43 F.R. 3254.

Appendix 10A
USDA Offices of
Investigation

Offenses relating to the agricultural industry are investigated by the U.S. Department of Agriculture. Its key executive officials in Washington are:

Office of the Inspector General
Independence Avenue and 14th Street, S.W.
Washington, D.C. 20250

Office of Audits
Independence Avenue and 14th Street, S.W.
Washington, D.C. 20250

Office of Investigation
Independence Avenue and 14th Street, S.W.
Washington, D.C. 20250

The department also has a number of regional offices around the country.

Regional Director, Region I
Office of Investigation
U.S. Department of Agriculture
Room 1707–26 Federal Plaza
New York, NY 10007

Regional Director, Region II
Office of Investigation
U.S. Department of Agriculture
Room 432A, Federal Building
Hyattsville, MD 20782

Regional Director, Region III
Office of Investigation
U.S. Department of Agriculture
1447 Peachtree Street, N.E., Rm. 901
Atlanta, GA 30309

Regional Director, Region IV
Office of Investigation
U.S. Department of Agriculture
1 North Wacker Drive, Rm. 800
Chicago, IL 60606

Regional Director, Region V
Office of Investigation
U.S. Department of Agriculture
101 South Main, Room 311
Federal Office Building
Temple, TX 76501

Regional Director, Region VI
Office of Investigation
U.S. Department of Agriculture
P.O. Box 205
Kansas City, MO 64141

Regional Director, Region VI
Office of Investigation
U.S. Department of Agriculture
555 Battery Street, Rm. 526
San Francisco, CA 94111

11 Defense, with Billions to Spend

A Michigan company wants to sell uniforms to the American army. An attorney for a Florida contractor wants to review possible breaches in his client's contract with the navy, and an Arizona businessman wants to find out how he can bid on an air force contract. With an annual budget in the hundreds of billions of dollars, and an employee force of several million men and women, the U.S. Department of Defense (DOD) constitutes a multibillion-dollar annual market for the private sector. DOD is one of the more important of the executive departments.

How DOD Operates

DOD is primarily responsible for ensuring the military security of the United States; its key officials are housed at the Pentagon. DOD, however, is not a monolith; rather, it is a decentralized and very large agency that employs more than one million civilians; two million men and women on active military duty; and one million men and women reservists.

The DOD consists of many agencies; among the more important ones are the Departments of the Army, Navy, and Air Force. The needs, politics, and constituencies of these agencies vary. Understanding their needs and knowing who their decision makers are can prove of value to anyone who does (or plans to do) business with DOD.

The depeartment was established under the National Security Act of 1947 (as amended in 1949).[1] Its titular chief officer is the President. However, the DOD's daily policies, direction, and management are the responsibility of the Secretary of Defense. It is the task of the Joint Chiefs of Staff to provide the secretary with the needed military technical assistance. The DOD Secretary is also assisted by the Secretaries of the Army, Navy, and Air Force.

The daily running of DOD operations rests with its Office of the Secretary. Within this office are found DOD's more important decision makers. Among these are the:

Deputy Secretary of Defense;

Special Assistant;

143

Undersecretary for Defense Policy;

Assistant Secretaries for Defense (of which there are seven);

Undersecretary of Defense for Research and Engineering; and

General Counsel

There are also agencies that can be of assistance to someone dealing with DOD. Remember, however, that each of these other agencies has its own internal politics, constituencies, and turf. The highly complex and decentralized structure of DOD necessitates that you communicate your inquiries to the agency with specific jurisdiction. The Departments of the Army, Navy, and Air Force each have their own secretaries who often rule their departments like personal fiefdoms. Turn to the Secretary of DOD only when all else fails; initially approach the staff of the particular agency that concerns you. If you go over their heads you may alienate them.

Important Officials at DOD

The Secretary of Defense is the most powerful official at DOD; the scope of the secretary's powers is detailed in the various provisions of the National Security Act.[2] The secretary, however, is a political animal; much of his time is consumed by the political environment and the President's policies. The daily work at the DOD is thus handled by its Deputy Secretary and Special Assistant Secretary. These two officers are also the DOD's contacts with the White House staff; the Special Assistant also serves as the secretary of the Armed Forces Policy Council, and advises both the Defense Secretary and the Deputy Secretary on important policies that can impact on the department's congressional dealings.

Another important official at the DOD is its Comptroller; he is the department's liaison with the Office of Management and Budget, the Congress, the General Accounting Office, and the other non-DOD agencies. The Comptroller also supervises, directs, and reviews the preparation and execution of the department's annual budget. His office exerts great influence over all matters connected to the DOD budget.

The Undersecretary for Defense Policy can also prove to be a valuable source when dealing with the DOD. He handles all departmental matters that are of a political nature, for example:

Arms limitations;

Arms negotiations;

Intelligence analysis;

Collection requirements;

Communications;

Command and control;

Use of outer space; and

Integration of departmental plans and policies.

The undersecretary also has jurisdiction over the Civil Defense Preparedness Agency (CDPA).

Legal matters are handled by the department's General Counsel (GC) and his staff. It is this office which advises officials on legal issues of import to the DOD. The GC is also responsible for preparing, processing, and reviewing all DOD-connected legislation, rules, and regulations. The GC staff is responsible for reviewing all DOD executive orders, proclamations, reports, and contracts. All DOD-related legal inquiries should be addressed to the GC staff.

When dealing with DOD officials, be sure to be armed with some knowledge of the workings of the department. Temper your knowledge with courtesy and discretion. Further, when presenting a case or position before the DOD bureaucracy, do so with confidence and authority; be sure of your facts. The DOD has its own pecking order; the old-boy network continues to influence many decisions. Bureaucrats in general will refrain from taking on someone who both understands the workings of the process and knows when and how to apply the pressure; however, pressure should be applied with tact and only as a last resort.

How the Joint Chiefs of Staff (JCS) Work

The JCS consists of a chairman and the Chiefs of Staff for the Departments of the Army, Navy, and Air Force; the Commandant of the Marine Corps is also invited to attend meetings of the JCS. The JCS are the principal military advisers to the President and the Secretary of Defense. In addition they perform the following important tasks.

Review the material, personnel, and logistic requirements of the military.

Establish the training and educational requirements for the military.

Advise the Secretary of DOD on the nation's military requirements.

Prepare the strategic plans and provisions of the military.

Review the plans and programs of the military commanders.

In turn, the JCS are assisted by the Joint Staff (JS), which numbers more than 300 military officers. These are selected from all three branches of the military. While the JCS develop policy, it is the JS that is responsible for ensuring that much of the routine daily work is carried out.

The JCS can (and often do) exercise power within DOD and also with key congressional committees. In this they are assisted by several important DOD agencies. Among these are the Defense Communications Agency; Defense Nuclear Agency; Defense Mapping Agency; and Defense Intelligence Agency. The JCS are often influential in decisions dealing with weapons programs and procurements; routine decisions, however, are delegated to the JS.

To an outsider, the JCS appear to be a military bureaucracy that is insulated from the Washington political arena. This is far from the truth. The JCS are both responsive to and part of the political machinations in national defense that emanate from the White House and Congress. They have input with some powerful congressional figures (especially those who sit on committees with jurisdiction over DOD); thus, the JCS exert influence over national defense through indirect channels. They understand how to use the political process.

The JCS and their staffs, as well as the White House staff and the Office of the Secretary, constitute a powerful group in defense-related policies and issues. They can easily assist or defeat efforts to modify, amend, or initiate policy. Thus, whenever you are soliciting support for a position, be sure to arm yourself with concrete facts and figures; in addition, assess the positions and interests of the other players.

Dealing with the Air Force

The Department of the Air Force (AF) is the youngest of the services; it has its own secretary and powerful constituency. The secretary is directly responsible to (and within the jurisdiction of) the Secretary of DOD.[3] It is within the Office of the Secretary that many of the AF's important decisions are made.

The AF has three assistant secretaries who assist the AF Secretary. There is also an Assistant to the Secretary who is responsible for the daily management of the AF, and an Administrative Assistant who serves as an adviser to the AF Secretary. The AF has its own General Counsel (GC); he advises the AF Secretary and staff on all legal matters dealing with the department. It is this office that reviews and handles all rules and regulations, congressional legislative concerns, and other inquiries that deal with the AF. Two additional AF officials of whom you should also be aware are the Director of Information and the Director of Space Systems.

The AF also has a Chief of Staff (CS) who is the department's military adviser. The CS is a member of the JCS; he is assisted by a Vice-Chief of Staff and a special staff. The department has some specialized units which include the following.

Accounting and Finance Center: provides technical supervision and guidance to the department's Accounting and Finance Division.

Audit Agency: carries out all AF internal audits.

Inspection and Safety Center: inspects and reviews the department's safety programs.

Office of Special Investigation: is the criminal-investigation arm of the AF and doubles as a counterintelligence bureau. The office also provides personnel security and other special investigatory services for the department.

Data Automation Agency: has jurisdiction over the department's centralized data-processing functions.

For additional information on these units, contact the AF's Director of Administration in Washington.

How the Army Runs

The Department of the Army (DA) is headed by a secretary who is responsible for its daily administration and policies;[4] the secretary is assisted by the:

Assistant Secretaries for:
  Civil Work;
  Installation, Logistics, and Financial Management;
  Manpower and Reserve Affairs;
  Research and Acquisition;

Undersecretary;

General Counsel;

Administrative Assistant; and

Chiefs of Legislative Liaison, and Public Affairs.

The department also has an Army Staff (AS) which is presided over by a Chief of Staff (CS). The functions of the AS are to:

Prepare the DA for deployment;

Organize, supply, equip, mobilize and demobilize the components of the DA;

Investigate and report on the efficiency of the DA;

Act as the representative of the DA Secretary; and

Act as the representative of the Joint Chiefs of Staff.

The department's CS also serves as the principal adviser to the Secretary of the DA. The CS is assisted by a personal staff which includes the Inspector General, the Director of the Army Staff, and several deputies. For additional information on the DA, contact its Office of Public Affairs in Washington.

How the Navy Sails

The Department of the Navy (DN) and the Office of the Secretary of the Navy were established by Congress in 1798.[5] The DN Secretary, like his counterparts in the army and air force, is assisted by a staff of several advisers. Among the more important are the Undersecretary, Deputy Undersecretary, General Counsel and Assistant Secretaries for:

Manpower, Reserve Affairs, and Logistics;

Financial Management; and

Research, Engineering, and Systems.

The DN also has a Judge Advocate General (JAG) who is the senior officer of the navy's Judge Advocate Corps. The JAG performs several important legal advisory functions; for example, the JAG:

Oversees the DN's legal assistance to its personnel and their families;

Partakes in navy court martials;

Reviews investigations and claims against the navy;

Partakes in nonjudicial punishments; and

Supervises the overall administration of justice within the department.

Another important DN official is the Comptroller.[6] He is responsible for:

The financial management of the navy;

Budgetary and accounting matters;

Statistical reporting;

Internal navy audits; and

The general administrative organization of the department.

The department's Naval Materiel Compound and Bureau of Naval Personnel handle all inquiries about DN contracts and procurements. If you want additional information on the department, contact its Office of Information in Washington.

Other Important DOD Agencies

There are several additional DOD agencies that you should be aware of, including the following.

Defense Intelligence Agency (DIA): under the control of the Secretary of Defense, DIA is headed by a director who reports to the Chairman of the Joint Chiefs of Staff. DIA is responsible for the production and dissemination of defense-related intelligence information within DOD.[7]

Defense Investigative Service (DIS): created by the Secretary of DOD for the purpose of consolidating DOD investigative activities. DIS is headed by a director and is under the direct control of the General Counsel Office. DIS has ten regional offices; these conduct all DOD-related investigations and personnel security checks.[8]

Defense Logistics Agency (DLA): under the control of an assistant secretary of defense. DLA's function is to supply logistic support and services to the other DOD agencies.[9]

Defense Mapping Agency (DMA): under the control of the Undersecretary of Defense for Research and Engineering. DMA manages all DOD mapping, charting, and other related activities.[10]

Defense Nuclear Agency (DNA): headed by a director who is responsible to the Undersecretary of Defense for Research and Engineering. DNA is responsible for nuclear weapons research and testing.[11]

Defense Civil Preparedness Agency (DCPA): headed by the Undersecretary of Defense Policy. The DCPA was established for the purpose of developing and implementing an effective national civil-defense program. The agency also assists local governments in establishing their own disaster-preparedness programs.[12]

Defense Audit Service (DAS): headed by the Deputy Assistant Secretary of Defense for Audit who reports to the Comptroller of the DOD. DAS performs all internal DOD audits; these are carried out by its twelve regional offices.[13]

Defense Communications Agency (DCA): headed by an assistant secretary for defense. DCA's primary role is to maintain and provide engineering assistance for all DOD communications-system networks.[14]

Defense Contract Audit Agency (DCAA): headed by an assistant secretary of defense. DCAA's function is to conduct all needed contract-related audit functions for the DOD.[15]

Defense Security Assistance Agency (DSAA): headed by a director. DSAA's function is to supply military assistance to friendly foreign countries.[16]

Armed Service Board of Contract Appeals: hears all appeals from the final decisions of DOD contracting officers.[17] On appeal, the board will review (de novo) all the evidence. Board decisions are by a majority vote.

Army Corps of Engineers (ACE): a division of the Department of the Army, and headed by a chief engineer.[18] ACE's primary responsibility is to authorize the construction of dams, reservoirs, harbors, waterways, and locks. ACE is also responsible for the discharge of dredged materials in navigable waters. Public comments on any ACE proposed projects should be directd to its Office of Civil Works in Washington.

With an annual budget in the hundreds of billions of dollars, DOD has come to represent a large market for business, but for others is a black hole that wasted the taxpayer's precious dollars. Contracts in the billions of dollars are signed daily; DOD also openly solicits bids from the private sector for numerous goods and services. Anyone who deals (or plans to deal) with the DOD must understand how it functions, and how and by whom decisions are made.

For additional information of DOD, contact its Staff Assistant for Public Correspondence, Office of the Secretary of Defense in Washington.

Notes

1. See, 5 U.S.C. 101.
2. See, 76 Stat. 638, and 72 Stat. 514.
3. See, 10 U.S.C. 8010.
4. See, 5 U.S.C. 171.
5. See, 10 U.S.C. 5031.
6. See, 10 U.S.C. 5061.
7. See, DOD Directive 5105.21, dated August 1, 1961.
8. See, DOD Directive 5105.42, dated April 18, 1972.
9. DLA was established pursuant to authority vested in the Secretary of DOD.
10. DMA was established in 1972 under provisions of the National Security Act of 1947.
11. See, DOD Directive 5105.31.
12. See, 50 U.S.C. app. 2251 et seq.
13. See, DOD Directive 5105.48.
14. DCA was established by direction of the Secretary of DOD on May 12, 1960.
15. See, DOD Directive 5105.36, dated June 9, 1965.
16. See, DOD Directive 5105.38, dated August 11, 1971.
17. The board was established jointly by the Secretaries of the Army, Navy, and Air Force on March 20, 1962.
18. See, 33 U.S.C. 403 and 419.

12 Commerce Means Business

A businessman is considering opening an office in Paris; the president of a minicomputer corporation is looking for a Nigerian distributor, while an Ohio entrepreneur is looking for overseas markets for his new invention.

The U.S. Department of Commerce (DC) can probably help these people; it can supply them with some of the necessary marketing information, and even assist them in promoting their products overseas. The department can provide them with scientific and technical data; for example, a Houston-based company used the department's census data to develop its marketing plans, and a Los Angeles marketing firm was able to obtain a county-by-county tabulation of small companies that might be interested in purchasing and selling a client's products.

The department expends millions of dollars a year in an assortment of economic and technical studies. Some of these deal with potential foreign and domestic markets, while other DC studies deal with the availability of investment opportunities. Some department studies contain valuable statistical data on a variety of economic matters. Many of these are readily available upon request. The DC can be an important source of information on a broad range of economic matters; the public would do well to explore what it has to offer.

Structure and Organization

The DC[1] is headed by a secretary who is ultimately responsible for the department's running and policy making. The DC Secretary is assisted by an Undersecretary. There is also an Office of General Counsel within DC; it is responsible for supervising all departmental legal activities and is the DC Secretary's legal adviser.

Another important department officer is the Assistant Secretary for Administration. This official is responsible for the department's program evaluations; budget; personnel policies; administrative services; audit and finances; and automated data processing management.

The Assistant Secretary for Policy is also an important decision maker who advises the DC Secretary on policy-related issues. In turn, the Office of Chief Economist advises the DC Secretary and other high departmental officials on economic matters. The merchant marine is the province of the Assistant Secretary for Maritime Affairs. Tourism is the responsibility of the Assistant Secretary for Tourism.

Congressional legislation is managed in the Office of Congressional Affairs and Relations, while the Assistant Secretary for Communications and Information handles the department's telecommunication activities. When addressing an inquiry to the department, make sure it is addressed to the appropriate official to ensure that it will not be lost in the department's bureaucratic maze.

The department's functions are divided among its agencies; many of these operate and function in a quasi-autonomous manner. They often guard their turfs jealously. Understanding how they operate and their jurisdictions should prove of value to any person dealing with the department. Remember that the Washington insider often simply directs a client to the appropriate official or agency; many times you can do this yourself. By so doing, you will be able to save time and money.

The Department's Agencies and Offices

Economic Development Administration (EDA)

The administration was established as an agency of the department to create jobs in the private sector.[2] In an effort to stimulate the creation of jobs, the EDA administers several programs involving:

Public works, loans, and grants;

Economic adjustment assistance grants;

Business loans for industrial and commercial facilities;

Guarantees for private loans; and

Technical planning and research assistance.

Any business located in an urban area designated as a growth center is eligible for some of these EDA programs. For additional details on these, you should contact the EDA Office of Public Affairs in Washington.

EDA loans and grants are also available to businesses located (or planning to locate) in areas of the country with high unemployment; businesses with programs to create jobs in these designated areas can qualify for departmental grants and loans. The EDA also provides financial and technical assistance to businesses that have suffered economic losses as a result of foreign competition.

Industry and Trade Administration (ITA)

The ITA was established to stimulate American exports. The agency offers specialized technical assistance to individuals and companies that are engaging in international trade.

The agency performs many of its tasks through specialized bureaus. These can often prove of assistance to members of the public planning to do business overseas.

Bureau of Export Development (BED): provides businesspeople with marketing and promotional assistance, as well as current information on sales, trade, and potential markets in specific foreign countries. BED can prove of special value to anyone doing or planning to do business in the Near East.

Bureau of East–West Trade (BEWT): offers assistance to those who are doing or plan to do business with the Eastern Bloc. It can provide them with current trade and marketing information.

Bureau of Trade Regulation (BTR): processes applications for the import of duty-free educational, scientific, and cultural materials.

Bureau of International Economic Policy and Research (BIEPR): conducts studies of foreign markets, and makes its findings available to the business community.

Bureau of Domestic Business Development (BDBD): collects and stores data on specific domestic industries in such areas as production, consumption, capacity, taxation, labor, and inventories.

Bureau of Field Operations (BFO): publishes current information on various marketing and economic developments of interest to businessmen. For additional information on BFO, see the *Federal Register,* volume 42, page 64721.

Office of Minority Business Enterprise (OMBE)

The office was established by the Secretary of Commerce to develop and administer department programs aimed at assisting minority-owned businesses. The OMBE also selects and funds local private groups that provide direct management and technical assistance to minority-owned businesses. For additional information, contact OMBE's Information Center, Washington, D.C.

National Bureau of Standards (NBS)

The bureau was established by an act of Congress to provide measurement standards for the nation. Through several of its institutes, the NBS provides valuable technical and scientific data to the public. The following are among its more important vehicles.

> *Institute for Computer Science and Technology:* conducts research and publishes studies in the area of computer technology.

> *Institute for Basic Standards:* coordinates the domestic measurement systems with those of foreign countries.

> *Institute for Material Research:* publishes and distributes standard reference material.

> *Institute for Applied Technology:* provides advisory and research services in the areas of construction technology, consumer product performance, and testing of electronic components.

The NBS also maintains a large library; this is open to all members of the public. For additional information on the bureau, you should contact its Office of Technical Publications in Washington.

National Oceanic and Atmospheric
Administration (NOAA)

The NOAA was established for the purpose of funding and conducting oceanic research.[3] It also conducts research in the atmospheric sciences and physics; these studies are available to the public upon request. The NOAA provides weather forecasts, and issues hurricane, tornado, and flood warnings.

In addition, the NOAA provides grants to a number of educational institutions for research in the marine area. These studies are often available to the private sector, and can prove valuable. For additional information on the NOAA, contact its Office of Public Affairs in Washington.

Bureau of Census (BC)

The bureau was established by Congress for the purpose of conducting a census of the population every ten years.[4] BC collects and publishes a wide variety of statistical data of value to both businesspeople and professionals on such areas as:

Population shifts;

Developments in the housing industry;

Shifts in the agricultural sector;

Developments in state and local governments; and

Trends in the manufacturing sector.

The bureau also collects current statistics on foreign trade, imports, exports, and shipping. It issues periodic reports on retail and wholesale trade, and selected services. The BC publishes numerous catalogues and directories on a variety of subjects. For additional information, contact the bureau's Public Information Office in Washington.

Patent and Trademark Office (PTO)

This office was established by Congress to "promote the progress of the useful arts."[5] Each year the PTO registers and renews more than 35,000 trademarks. These include distinctive works, names, symbols, or devices that are used by manufacturers, businesspeople, and merchants to identify their goods and services. Trademarks are registered for twenty-one years and can be renewed.

The PTO also issues more than 17,000 patents each year. These often fall into one of the following three categories:

Designing patents (issued for three and one-half, seven, and fourteen years);

Plant patents (issued for seventeen years); and

Utility patents (issued for seventeen years).

The office records and indexes documents that transfer the ownership of patents and trademarks; and it maintains a scientific library of more than 2 million documents. It includes both domestic and foreign patents and trademarks. The office will also hear and decide on appeals from prospective inventors and trademark applicants; in addition, the PTO compiles a weekly list of all the patents and trademarks it has issued. For additional information, contact its Commissioner of Patents and Trademarks in Washington.

Bureau of Economic Analysis (BEA)

The bureau was established by the Secretary of Commerce; its primary function is to develop and intercept the economic accounts of the United

States.[6] These provide valuable information on the production, distribution, and use of the national output. BEA's economic accounts consist chiefly of the national income and product accounts. They also include wealth accounts; interindustry accounts; regional accounts; balance-of-payments accounts.

The bureau provides and publishes additional economic forecasts; for example:

Surveys of investment outlays and plants;

Plans of American business;

Econometric models of the economy; and

A system of economic indicators.

For additional information, contact the bureau's Information Services in Washington.

National and Technical Information Service (NTIS)

The NTIS serves as a clearinghouse for an array of technical data.[7] Its staff collects more than 60,000 new technical reports a year; it also has a library of more than 900,000 reports that deal with a multitude of technical areas. NTIS maintains a computerized bibliographic data file (of both published and unpublished scientific reports) of value to industry. In addition, the agency maintains a microfiche service which is available to the public.

Office of Telecommunications (OT)

The office was established for the purpose of funding and publishing studies in the area of telecommunications. The OT can also, upon request, provide information on such topics as:

Techniques employed to evaluate telecommunications systems;

Models for estimating telecommunications transmission characteristics; and

Applications of telecommunications.

The OT also performs in-depth research (of special value to communications firms) in several areas of telecommunications. These include engineering and evaluation of systems; electromagnetic wave transmission and services; efficient use of the spectrum; and telecommunications application.

The agencies of the DC can be a valuable resource for members of the public who are engaged in domestic or foreign economic activities. DC can also assist consultants, lawyers, and other professionals who have clients with an interest in these areas.

Notes

1. See, 15 U.S.C. 1501.

2. See, 42 U.S.C. 3121.

3. See, Title XVI, chapter 9 and Title XXXIII, chapter 17 of the U.S.C.

4. See, the *Federal Register,* volume 40, page 42765.

5. See, Article 1, Section 8 of the U.S. Constitution; see also, 25 U.S.C. 1–293, 35 U.S.C. 1, and 15 U.S.C. 1051.

6. See, the *Federal Register,* volume 40, page 42766.

7. See, 15 U.S.C. 115–117; also, the *Federal Register,* volume 41, page 10538.

13 Energy Means Megabucks

An energy exploration company in Oklahoma signed a multimillion-dollar contract with the U.S. Department of Energy (DOE). However, the DOE's Office of Equal Opportunity advised that the company had violated the Age Discrimination Employment Act. The company now stands to lose this important contract. In a separate case, a consulting firm finds itself consistently being outbidded by a competitor for DOE contracts; its management suspects foul play, but does not know what to do about it.

Energy resources are a diminishing commodity, and the DOE stands for megabucks. Understanding this important department's jurisdiction and organizational structure should enable anyone with an interest in the energy area to keep abreast of developments and have some form of input in DOE policymaking. For the businessman, who must be knowledgeable in federal energy-related rules and regulations, a grasp of DOE's operations is essential.

What DOE Does

One of the newest of the federal departments, the DOE was created under the Department of Energy Act (42 U.S.C. 7131). The act gave DOE jurisdiction over some of the energy-connected functions previously exercised by some of the other federal departments and agencies; for example, the Departments of the Interior, Commerce, Housing and Urban Development, and the Interstate Commerce Commission. DOE became a repository for many of the energy-related rules and regulations previously exercised in a fragmented manner by a multitude of agencies. It was hoped that this would help centralize and better coordinate the nation's energy policies.

Because of its broad jurisdiction, DOE funds a multitude of programs and studies; much of this information could prove of value to a businessperson or professional who is engaged in any energy-related industry. The following are some of the studies and projects that have been funded by DOE.

Production and consumption studies

Studies on the marketing of energy resources

Uses and implementation of solar power

Environmental-impact studies

Energy research and development projects

Studies on energy-related technologies

Resource application projects

Conservation programs

Nuclear energy and weapons studies

The DOE also contracts annually with the private sector for a multitude of services. The department plays a key role in the regulation of the production and use of energy-related resources. However, the DOE has come under criticism from both consumer and industry groups. The former have charged that the department has done too little to safeguard the interests of the consuming public; while the latter notes that the DOE's many rules and regulations have served to stifle initiatives by the private sector.

But the DOE has managed to learn the Washington survival game; efforts to abolish or restructure it have been fruitless. Unlike many of the other federal regulators, the DOE has proven to be a valuable resource for the energy industry. It has assisted the industry in marketing its products. The Washington insiders have learned how to tap DOE's kitty.

How Decisions Are Made

Understanding an agency's decision making is a must for anyone who deals with it; knowing who its key decision makers are can often make the difference between winning and losing. The DOE's key decision makers are its Secretary, Deputy Secretary, and its Undersecretary. These three individuals and their staffs are responsible for the planning, direction, and control of the department. In addition, the DOE Secretary serves as the president's chief adviser on energy-related matters, and is a cabinet official.

The Deputy Secretary represents the DOE's interests before Congress, and is also responsible for overseeing the Economic Regulatory Administration and the Energy Information Administration. The Undersecretary is the third member of this triumvirate; he oversees the DOE's programs and funding in the areas of solar energy, conservation, energy research, energy technology, and defense.

There are many other department officials who play important roles in operation and management. However, as with any bureaucracy, the real work at DOE is carried out by the staffs of these officials. It is often of great value to have ties to key members of the staff. They carry out the policies and programs of the DOE officialdom; they are the soldiers in the trenches. Knowing who they are and how they function can prove as important as knowing how the top leadership functions.

Important DOE Offices

On first contact, the DOE appears to be a labyrinth; it can, by its sheer size and numerous agencies and divisions, intimidate an outsider. However, knowing which DOE office or division can assist you with a problem can often prove as valuable as knowing its key players.

The *Office (of the Assistant Secretary) for Policy and Evaluation (OPE)* formulates the DOE's overall domestic energy policy. The OPE also conducts studies of domestic energy needs and advises the DOE Secretary on energy-related congressional legislation.

The *Office (of the Assistant Secretary) for Intergovernmental and Industrial Relations (OIIR)* handles the department's consumer-related concerns and serves as the DOE's contact for consumer groups. The OIIR also oversees the DOE's relations with congressional committees, the press, and private business groups.

The *Office (of the Assistant Secretary) for International Affairs (OIA)* has jurisdiction over the department's international programs. The OIA also oversees the DOE's international agreements and advises the DOE Secretary and the White House on international energy-related developments. The agency studies oil supplies and pricing trends, and communicates with foreign government agencies and international groups on numerous concerns.

The *Office of General Counsel (OGC)* is the department's legal adviser. It advises top DOE officials, divisions, and agencies on congressional legislation, interpretations of rules and regulations, the legality of departmental programs and contracts, and its patent program. The OGC also represents the DOE in all civil and administrative litigation, and plays an important role in any decision to refer DOE investigations to the Department of Justice for prosecution. (The Federal Energy Regulatory Commission, however, has an independent counsel.)

The *Office of Inspector General (OIG)* is the department's in-house policeman. The OIG conducts and supervises all DOE-related civil and criminal investigations; it also oversees all DOE and Federal Energy Regulatory Commission internal audits, and identifies infractions of departmental rules and regulations. All enforcement actions must be approved by the DOE Secretary.

The Office of the Controller (OC) oversees and manages the DOE's finances. This office also administers the department's loan-guarantee programs.

The *Office of Equal Opportunity (OEO)* administers and oversees DOE civil-rights policies and programs. The director of the OEO also serves as an adviser to the DOE Secretary on equal employment opportunity and civil-rights-related matters. The OEO oversees the civil-rights policies and practices of all private corporations and individuals that receive DOE funds.

The *Office of Energy Research (OER)* oversees DOE research and development programs, and also provides funding for private groups that are engaged in energy-related research. In addition, the OER monitors domestic and international energy-research programs.

The *Office for Energy and Technology (OET)* has responsibility for overseeing the department's solar, geothermal, fossil, and nuclear programs. The OET also has an interest in areas related to the application of new technologies and potential energy resources.

The *Office for Resource Application (ORA)* has responsibility for all DOE efforts to increase domestic petroleum, natural gas, coal, and uranium supplies. The ORA manages the department's resource-leasing programs, and administers the following.

1. Alaska Power Administration
2. Bonneville Power Administration
3. Southeastern Power Administration
4. Southwestern Power Administration
5. Western Area Power Administration
6. Naval Petroleum Reserves and Oil Shale Reserves
7. Strategic Petroleum Reserves

The *Office for Conservation and Solar Applications (OCSA)* directs the department's conservation and solar commercialization programs. The OCSA oversees DOE domestic energy-conservation efforts, and renders assistance to private groups in this area.

The *Office for Environment (OE)* ensures that departmental programs are in compliance with all federal environmental laws and regulations. This office is also responsible for reviewing all departmental environmental-impact statements.

The *Office for Defense Programs (ODP)* directs all DOE nuclear weapons research, testing, and production programs. The ODP oversees the department's classification and declassification of sensitive nuclear-related data.

The *Economic Regulatory Administration (ERA)* is responsible for the administration of all DOE regulatory programs. The ERA is also charged with ensuring compliance with DOE rules and regulations regarding crude oil, petroleum products, natural gas liquids, natural gas import/export controls, and emergency and contingency planning. The ERA represents the DOE before the Federal Energy Regulatory Commission.

The *Energy Information Administration (EIA)* has responsibility for the collection and publication of data on energy reserves and the finances of energy companies. The EIA is also responsible for departmental dealings with the production, demand, and consumption of energy; in addition, it prepares departmental studies on long-term energy trends and conducts field audits.

The *Federal Energy Regulatory Commission (FERC)* is an independent, five-member body which has assumed many of the powers previously held by the Federal Power Commission. The FERC has power to set rates; transport charges; regulate the sale of electricity; license hydroelectric plants; and set charges for the transport of oil by pipeline.

The *Office of Hearings and Appeals (OHA)* reviews all orders issued by the other DOE agencies, except for those which fall within the jurisdiction of the FERC. The OHA has power to review all requests by private individuals and groups for exemptions from the department's regulations.

The DOE and its offices are responsible for the regulation and coordination of many of this country's energy needs; few in the private sector are not affected by its rules and regulations. The department serves diverse and powerful constituencies. Understanding how it functions and operates is important in an energy-hungry society. For additional information, contact DOE's Office of the Secretary in Washington.

14 Justice, the Boys with the Big Stick

A Denver businessman is indicted for securities fraud; his attorney argues that his client was promised immunity by the staff of the U.S. Securities and Exchange Commission. In another instance, the president and general counsel for a Boston electronics firm met with attorneys for the U.S. Department of Justice (DOJ) in Washington. A disgruntled employee had tipped off the department's Fraud Section that the company had made illegal corporate payments to a member of Congress. A food distributor was the target of a well-conceived extortion scheme; he wanted to know where he could turn for assistance.

The DOJ is the nation's largest law firm; it employs more than 1,500 attorneys, has an annual budget in the billions of dollars, and has jurisdiction over the federal criminal code. The department also represents many of the other federal agencies in civil litigation; it renders legal advice and opinions to the White House and the heads of the executive departments. Some of the nation's largest criminal-investigation bodies are found in the DOJ.

How the Department Runs

The Office of Attorney General (AG) is the nation's chief law-enforcement officer; he is also the President's chief legal adviser.[1] The importance of this office has varied with the person occupying it, and also with the administration in power. Many AGs have, unfortunately, been ill-equipped for the task. The office, however, can be an important position when occupied by someone who knows and understands the parameters of power.

Power and responsibility are divided among DOJ's many divisions; each of these is headed by an assistant attorney general. Within DOJ are also found several important law-enforcement agencies. Each of the divisions and agencies has been delegated a specified role within the federal law-enforcement apparatus. However, all of these are ultimately responsible to the AG.

The real power in the department rests with a small number of officials, all of whom report to the AG. Each of these plays an important role in running and formulating policy at DOJ.

The *Deputy Attorney General (DAG)* is the second most powerful official at DOJ, and directly assists the AG. The DAG plays an important role in matters that relate to the department's criminal prosecutorial decisions and policies. In addition, he is responsible for all Freedom of Information and Privacy Act appeals as they relate to the department.

The *Associate Attorney General (AAG)* has primary jurisdiction over the department's civil cases and policies; he also assists the AG in administering the department. The AAG is responsible for screening all federal judicial candidates and political appointments at the department. In addition, he is in charge of DOJ's hiring policies and oversees the department's legal staff.

The *Solicitor General (SG)* represents the department before the U.S. Supreme Court. He also plays an important role in deciding which cases the department should appeal to the Court.

The *Legal Counsel (LC)* office is occupied by an Assistant Attorney General who acts as the AG's legal adviser. He handles legal questions directed to the department by other executive agencies and the White House staff. The LC resolves all legal disputes between the federal agencies; he also reviews all proposed executive orders and proclamations, and departmental rules and regulations.

The *Legislative Affairs (LA)* office is held by an assistant attorney general who is responsible for the coordination and handling of all departmental congressional inquiries and legislation. The LA also comments on all legislation that emanates from DOJ or the other executive agencies.

The *Pardon Attorney (PA)* reviews, investigates, and comments on all pardon applications.

The *Counsel on Professional Responsibility (CPR)* oversees and investigates all charges of misconduct filed against DOJ employees. If the CPR finds that an employee has violated the law or a DOJ regulation, it can:

Refer the matter to the appropriate DOJ division or agency for disposition; or

Recommend that the AG's office take direct and appropriate action.

The *Counsel for Intelligence Policy (CIP)* advises the AG on all intelligence-related DOJ activities. The CIP prepares and files all applications for surveillance under the Foreign Intelligence Surveillance Act. The CIP works closely with the intelligence community in developing legislative proposals, and provides advise on legal matters that impact on intelligence activities. In addition CIP advises the DOJ, the Defense

Department, the State Department, and the intelligence agencies on the legality of proposed rules, regulations, and guidelines for domestic and foreign intelligence operations.

The *Office for Legal Policy (OLP)* is headed by an assistant attorney general. The OLP reviews and advises the department on legislation that impacts on law enforcement and correctional institutions. The OLP manages and coordinates the department's responsibilities under the Freedom of Information and Privacy Acts; it also advises the AG on the selection and appointment of federal judges.

The *Trustee Program (TP)* was established under the Bankruptcy Reform Act of 1978 as a pilot project in eighteen federal judicial districts.[2] The DOJ Trustees are appointed by the AG and supervise the administration of bankruptcy cases; performance of private trustees in individual cases; proceedings under chapter 7; reorganization proceedings under chapter 11; and adjustment of debits under chapter 13. The Trustees have authority to appoint creditors' committees in chapter 11 proceedings.

The *Assistant Attorney General for Administration (AAGA)* heads the department's Justice Management Division. The AAGA assists the department's officials and divisions in areas related to:

Auditing;

Budget and financial management;

Personnel training and management;

Security;

Records management; and

Equal-opportunity programs.

What the Divisions Do

The department's responsibilities for enforcing the federal laws have been delegated to its divisions. It is the divisions that handle much of the department's litigation.

Criminal Divison (CD)

The CD is responsible for enforcing the federal criminal code, except for those statutes specifically designated to the department's other divisions. CD attorneys work closely with the ninety-five U.S. attorney offices, and also assist the Solicitor General's staff in preparing legal briefs in criminal appeals before the Supreme Court.

The CD is divided into sections; these carry out many of its important functions:

1. *Internal Security (IS):* has responsibility for enforcing federal criminal statutes that affect national security. The IS also administers the Foreign Agents Registration Act.
2. *Organized Crime and Racketeering (OCR):* is responsible for directing the department's organized-crime investigations and prosecutions.
3. *Fraud:* directs the department's efforts in the area of white-collar crime.
4. *Public Integrity (PI):* coordinates the DOJ's anticorruption programs aimed at local, state, and federal elected officials.
5. *International Affairs (IA):* handles the DOJ's international extradition proceedings, and has jurisdiction over international criminal-justice enforcement policies.
6. *Narcotics and Dangerous Drugs (NDD):* directs and coordinates federal prosecutorial efforts directed at high-level drug dealers.
7. *Office of Legislation (OL):* reviews and comments on congressional criminal statutes.
8. *Appellate Office (AO):* handles the division's appeals before the eleven U.S. courts of appeal and also the Supreme Court.
9. *Legal Support Services (LSS):* processes immunity and tax disclosure requests from the U.S. attorney offices. The LSS also coordinates the collection of criminal fines and bond forfeiture judgments.
10. *Office of Enforcement Operations (OEO):* oversees the department's use of electronic surveillance, witness relocation programs, and confidential funds.
11. *Office of General Litigation and Legal Advice (OGLLA):* provides specialized litigation support for the division and the U.S. attorney offices.

The CD has broad jurisdiction (which it often shares with the U.S. attorneys) in the following areas.

Violations of the federal bank statutes

Kidnapping

Aircraft hijackings

Frauds against the federal government or federal programs

Mail, wire, bankruptcy, or election frauds

Bribery of federal officials, or foreign officials[3]

Theft and embezzlement of federal property

Interstate transportation of stolen motor vehicles

Illegal transportation of firearms and explosives

Crimes on the high seas

Crimes on federal reservations

Violations in fishing conservation laws

Protection of the Continental Shelf resources

Criminal statutes dealing with labor unions and their pension and welfare funds

The division also has (together with the U.S. attorneys) jurisdiction over the following.

Immigrations and nationality laws

Offers in compromise in pending criminal cases under the tax laws (dealing with liquor and narcotics)

Civil litigation dealing with prisoners rights and parole procedures

Federal criminal legislative proposals

Subversive activities (for example: treason, sabotage, espionage, sedition,)

Appeals from rulings of the Drug Enforcement Administration

In addition, the CD has direct responsibility for enforcing specific federal laws. These are as follows.

1. Neutrality Statutes[4]
2. Arms Export Control Act
3. Contraband Transportation Act
4. Federal Aviation Act
5. Export Control Act
6. Federal Alcohol Administration Act
7. Controlled Substances Act
8. Atomic Energy Act
9. Trading with the Enemy Act[5]

10. Selective Service Act[6]
11. Foreign Agents Registration Act[7]
12. Federal regulation of Lobbying Act[8]
13. Executive Order No. 10450

The division also renders advisory opinions to the federal agencies on matters that relate to internal security.

Antitrust Division (AD)

This division is responsible for enforcing the federal antitrust laws. The AD staff investigates potential antitrust violations, conducts grand jury proceedings, and handles all antitrust-related appeals. The division also negotiates settlements and enforces all antitrust-related consent orders. In addition, it has both criminal and civil jurisdiction over cases involving restraints and monopolization of trade.

The AD reviews the orders of the Interstate Commerce Commission, the Federal Communications Commission, and the Nuclear Regulatory Commission, to ensure that these are in compliance with the federal antitrust laws. Further, it participates in all cases the Federal Trade Commission brings before the Supreme Court.

The division has broad jurisdiction over all activities that seriously impact on competition in the private sector. For example it has jurisdiction over:

Licensing of nuclear power reactors;

Interstate oil compacts;

Disposal of federally owned surplus property;

Proposed bank mergers;

Defense programs;

Federal patent policies;

Satellite communication policies; and

Foreign trade policies.

In addition, it can intervene in any regulatory proceedings conducted by the Interstate Commerce Commission; Civil Aeronautics Board; and Securities and Exchange Commission. The AD also has a Consumer Affairs Section which is empowered to enforce all consumer-related orders and rules enacted by the Federal Communications Commission; Food and Drug Administration; and Federal Trade Commission.

Civil Division (CD)

This division handles the department's civil litigation, except for some specialized civil litigation handled by the department's other divisions. The head of the CD is an assistant attorney general. The division has jurisdiction over the following areas.

Suits and claims filed by or against the government

Injunctive actions filed against cabinet members, agency heads, and other federal officials

Civil actions brought to enforce federal laws

Tort actions

The division also has primary jurisdiction over the following.

Admiralty and shipping civil proceedings either by or against the government

U.S. Court of Claims cases

U.S. Customs Court proceedings

Civil actions brought under the False Claims Act

Civil fraud cases

Patent, copyright, and trademark cases

Alien property cases

Suits under the Walsh–Healey Act

Treble damage claims under the Elkins Act

Freedom of Information and Privacy Act cases

Taft–Hartley and Labor–Management Reporting and Disclosure Acts suits

Federal suits in state courts

Federal civil appeals

In addition, the division has jurisdiction over all cases brought in foreign courts by or against the federal government. It is responsible for litigation involving the Department of Housing and Urban Development.

Tax Division (TD)

The TD has jurisdiction over all criminal and civil prosecutions arising under the federal tax laws, except for cases before the U.S. Tax Court. The latter are handled by the legal staff of the Internal Revenue Service (IRS). The TD is responsible for the following.

Defending the federal government in tax refund actions

Representing the Departments of Defense and Energy in state and local tax cases

Bringing lawsuits to foreclose federal tax liens and to collect upaid assessments

Filing civil suits against delinquent taxpayers

Bringing lawsuits to establish federal tax claims in bankruptcy, receivership, or probate cases

Defending all lawsuits brought against the IRS

Handling all Freedom of Information and Privacy Act lawsuits filed against the IRS

The division also has primary jurisdiction over criminal prosecutions involving tax evasion; willful failure to file a tax return; willful failure to pay taxes; and filing of a false tax return.

The division (like the other DOJ divisions) works closely with the U.S. attorney offices in many of its cases. In fact because the division's resources are limited, many of the department's criminal tax prosecutions are handled by the federal attorney offices. The division also works closely with the IRS.

Civil Rights Division (CRD)

The CRD is responsible for enforcing all federal civil-rights laws; the division has jurisdiction over the civil-rights criminal statutes.[9] In addition, the CRD's staff undertakes its own investigations, conducts negotiations, and handles all civil-rights enforcement proceedings.

Land and Natural Resources Division (LNRD)

LNRD is responsible for enforcing all federal laws dealing with the government's interest in real property and natural resources. For example it deals with actions to:

Remove clouds and quiet title;

Recover damages for trespass;

Recover possession of property;

Cancel patents;

Determine boundries;

Establish mineral rights; and

Safeguard water resources.

The division has jurisdiction over all criminal prosecutions emanating from federal water, air, and land pollution interests. In addition, it is responsible for representing the administrator of the Environmental Protection Agency in suits involving judicial review of that agency's actions. The division also defends lawsuits brought under the Surface Mining Control and Reclamation Act, and the National Environmental Policy Act.

How the Bureaus Operate

The bureaus have an important national law-enforcement function. In many ways, they resemble the autonomous regulatory agencies. These bureaus are important components of the department; without them it could not perform its assigned tasks.

The *Federal Bureau of Investigation (FBI)* is the best known of the federal law-enforcement agencies in the nation. It has broad investigatory powers. The FBI is authorized to carry out investigations in the following areas.

Domestic security cases (for example, espionage and sabotage)

Interstate transportation of stolen property

Robberies of federally insured banks

Interstate gambling and extortion schemes

Organized-crime activities

Frauds against the government

Killing of a federal official

White-collar crimes that impact on interstate and Foreign commerce

The *Marshals Service (MS)* consists of more than 1,500 deputies and 94 marshals. Under the Organized Crime Control Act of 1970, the MS has jurisdiction over the witness-protection program in organized-crime cases. The MS is also authorized to:

Provide physical security for the federal courts;

Protect federal judges, court personnel, and jurors;

Execute all federal civil and criminal processes;

Maintain custody of and transport federal prisoners; and

Safeguard all funds and property seized by federal agents.

The *Immigration and Naturalization Service (INS)* is responsible for administering the U.S. immigration and naturalization laws.[10] The INS is also authorized to:

Admit and exclude nonresident aliens;

Handle deportation proceedings;

Determine the admissibility of aliens into this country; and

Examine alien petitions for permanent residency and citizenship.

The *Board of Immigration Appeals (BIA)* is a quasi-judicial agency which enjoys great autonomy. The BIA has nationwide jurisdiction to hear appeals from INS decisions; it is comprised of a chairman and four members and is completely independent of the INS. The BIA hears appeals from:

Orders in INS administrative hearings;

Decisions in INS deportation hearings;

Decisions of exclusion proceedings;

Orders of the INS district directors;

Orders imposing administrative fines on carriers; and

Motions to reopen and reconsider provious decisions.

The *Bureau of Prisons (BP)* operates and administers the federal corrections system. The BP also issues standards and guidelines for the administration of the system.

The *U.S. Board of Parole* consists of nine members and has sole authority to grant, modify, deny, or revoke the parole of a federal prisoner who is serving a sentence in excess of one year. The board is also authorized to supervise those federal prisoners who are on parole; it determines, under authority given it by the Labor Management Reporting and Disclosure Act, whether someone convicted of labor racketeering activity can serve as a labor-union official again. In addition, the board is authorized under the Employment Retirement Income Act to determine if such persons will be allowed to work for, or provide services to employment benefit plans. These laws are aimed at shutting the doors of labor unions to convicted felons with ties to organized crime.

The *Drug Enforcement Administration (DEA)* combines all federal antinarcotic efforts under one umbrella. DEA is authorized to enforce the federal narcotics laws; the bureau is also responsible for regulating the legal narcotic market. DEA does this by:

Enacting import–export quotas for narcotics and other dangerous drugs;

Registering all authorized narcotic dealers;

Inspecting the premises and records of drug manufacturers; and

Investigating instances of criminal diversion.

DOJ is an umbrella organization covering a number of other agencies. Each of these has its own rules, regulations, and bureaucratic politics; some operate in a quasi-autonomous manner. Their own internal interests hinder the department's efforts to carry out the policies of the administration in power. Anyone who has to deal with DOJ should understand the likes and dislikes of the staff. It is the bureaucrats who really rule at DOJ. For additional information on the department, contact its Office of Public Information in Washington

Notes

1. See, 28 U.S.C. 501 and 503.
2. See, 11 U.S.C. 101.

3. See, 15 U.S.C. 78dd–1, 78dd–2, and 78ff.

4. See, 18 U.S.C. 956 et seq.

5. See, 50 U.S.C. app. 5(b).

6. See, 50 U.S.C. 451 et seq.

7. See, 22 U.S.C. 611 et seq.

8. See, 2 U.S.C. 261, and 46 U.S.C. 1225. In addition, for prohibitions against government employees acting as agents of foreign nations, see 18 U.S.C. 219; for prohibitions against domestic political contributions by foreign nationals, see 2 U.S.C. 441.

9. See, 18 U.S.C. 241, 242, and 245.

10. See, *Code of Federal Regulations,* Title VIII, part 100.

15

At Labor, Employees and Employers Compete

A California-based company agreed to a $300,000 settlement with the U.S. Department of Labor (DOL) stemming from charges that it had discriminated against the handicapped in its hiring practices. The company also agreed to improve its job-placement efforts in the recruiting and hiring of the handicapped. In another case, the DOL staff asked the Department of Justice to consider criminal prosecution in a case stemming from the death of an employee of a chemical company; the employee had been killed in a chemical explosion at one of the company's plants. If convicted, the management could face prison terms of up to six months and/or fines of up to $10,000.

The role of the federal government has become pervasive in our modern economy; it has made little difference which of the two political parties has been in power. The powers of government have expanded with the demands placed on it by an industrial society. Congress has, in large part, reacted to these pressures; ensuring the health, welfare, and privacy of a workforce of more than 110 million men and women has resulted in a maze of rules and regulations.

To ensure that its mandate is carried out, Congress has authorized the DOL to regulate and police employer–employee relations; Congress has also created several other agencies to assist in this task. The DOL, in turn, has assigned this task to its bureaus and divisions.

The DOL is one of the more important executive departments; its everyday decisions have an impact on every facet of our society. No employer or employee escapes its reach. For example, the Occupational Safety and Health Administration (OSHA) carries out more than 50,000 annual inspections; it also investigates complaints by employees that deal with the health and safety of their workplace. At DOL, employers and employees compete.

How Decisions Are Made

The DOL[1] administers more than 120 federal laws dealing with a multitude of employee-connected issues. By law, the DOL is authorized to regulate and police such employer-employee issues as:

179

Minimum hourly wages;

Overtime pay;

Hiring practices;

Unemployment insurance;

Workers' compensation and pensions; and

Labor–management relations.

As with any large bureaucracy, decisions at the DOL are made by a large number of individuals. The key policy decisions, however, are made by a small number of officials.

The DOL Secretary heads the department, and is also the President's principal adviser on labor matters. Traditionally, the office has been held by someone closely tied to labor management. However, this is not a fixed rule; some Presidents have been known to appoint individuals who have had little or no ties to labor unions. The Undersecretary is the principal adviser to the secretary.

The Solicitor heads the DOL's legal staff and is its legal adviser. His office both coordinates and litigates many of the civil and criminal prosecutions brought by the DOL staff under the following acts.

Occupational Safety and Health Act

Employee Retirement Security Act

Fair Labor Standards Act

Longshoremen's and Harbor Workers Compensation Act

Farm Labor Contractor Registration Act

The solicitor's staff also represents the department in all its administrative hearings; its criminal prosecutions, however, are handled by the Department of Justice (DOJ). DOL appeals are handled by the solicitor's headquarters office in Washington, while the regional cases are handled by its field offices.

An Inspector General (IG) handles all DOL investigations. The IG's staff also conducts audits and investigates allegations of fraud, theft, and waste in the DOL programs. The IG is responsible for investigating allegations of fraud and theft involving labor-union pension and welfare funds; criminal cases are referred to the DOJ, since the IG is not a criminal investigative agency.

The Director of Information, Publication and Reports is responsible for the DOL's information and publication programs. The director is the department's de facto public-relations officer. This office is a valuable source of information on how the DOL works and its program and publications.

Another important official is the Assistant Secretary for Administration and Management. He is responsible for the daily administrative operations of the DOL and its agencies. This official also handles matters dealing with equal employment opportunity.

There is also a Deputy Undersecretary for Legislation and Intergovernmental Relations who reviews the impact of the DOL programs and policies on the welfare and health of workers; while the Deputy Undersecretary for International Affairs is in charge of the DOL's international programs and dealings.

Administrative Hearings

Within the DOL are found several quasi-judicial agencies; these hear and resolve disputes involving the department, employers, and employees. These hearings deal with disputes that arise under one or more of the statues, rules, and regulations over which the DOL has jurisdiction. The resolution of these disputes lies with three offices.

1. The Office of Administrative Law Judges *(ALJ):* presides over all DOL administrative hearings. At the conclusion of every administrative hearing, the ALJ will submit findings and recommendations to either the DOL Secretary or one of his assistants.

The ALJ has jurisidiction over all disputes dealing with minimum wage requirements, overtime payments, and compensation payments. The ALJ also has jurisdiction to hear all cases dealing with health and safety regulations arising under any of the following.

1. Longshoremen's and Harbor Workers Compensation Act
2. Contract Work Hours and Safety Standards Act
3. Walsh–Healey Public Contract Act
4. McNamara–O'Hara Service Contract Act
5. Davis–Bacon Act
6. Occupational Safety and Health Act
7. Fair Labor Standards Act
8. Farm Labor Contractor Registration Act
9. Executive Order No. 11491
10. Black Lung Benefits Act
11. Social Security Act

The ALJ also constitutes a permanent Board of Contract Appeals.

2. The Employees Compensation Appeals Board (ECAB): consists of three members, one of whom acts as its chairman. They are appointed by the DOL Secretary. ECAB hears and renders decisions on all appeals that arise under the Federal Employees Compensation Act.[2] The ECAB decisions are final and are not subject to judicial review.

3. The Benefits Review Board (BRB) is a three-member, quasi-judicial body. The board exclusive jurisdiction over all appeals arising under the Longshoremen's and Harbor Workers Compensation Act and the Black Lung Benefits Act.[3]

How Agencies and Bureaus Operate

The DOL has a multitude of quasi-autonomous bureaus and agencies; these play important specialized roles in the employer–employee regulatory framework.

Labor-Management Services Administration (LMSA)

This agency is headed by an administrator, and is responsible for regulating veteran reemployment rights. The LMSA is authorized to assist military reservists and veterans in the exercise of their remployment rights.[4] It can refer an employer who refuses to reemploy a reservist or veteran (at a position, seniority, status, and rate of pay they would have received had they not entered the military) to the DOJ for prosecution. Few of these cases, however, are referred for prosecution; efforts to resolve reemployment disputes are usually handled on a voluntary basis. Upon request, the LMSA will supply you with reemployment information.

The LMSA also regulates the Labor–Management Reporting Act which requires labor unions to file with the LMSA copies of their constitutions, bylaws, and annual reports; these are open for public review. The LMSA is also authorized to police the election of union officials, as well as the handling of union funds by the officials. The agency is authorized to bring a civil suit in federal court to enforce compliance with its regulations.

The Employee Retirement Income Security Act (ERISA) requires the administrators of private pension and welfare plans to file copies of their plans with the LMSA.[5] It also requires them to report to the LMSA the financial status of those plans on an annual basis. ERISA requires that all plan participants be provided with periodic summaries of the plans and that their administrators be bonded. The LMSA Administrator is authorized to take all necessary steps to ensure compliance with this act.

LMSA is authorized to supervise union elections, investigate all member grievances, and decide on the appropriate bargaining unit, under Executive Order No. 11491. The order also requires federal employee unions to file annual reports with the LMSA, and take adequate measures to ensure that their elections will be fair. The LMSA is authorized to take all necessary steps to ensure that union funds will be properly administered. The agency also keeps the DOL abreast of national labor-management disputes, and negotiators involved in collective bargaining.

Occupational Safety and Health Administration (OSHA)

OSHA is headed by the Assistant Secretary for Occupational Safety and Health.[6] The agency is charged with developing and promulgating occupational and health standards, and workplace rules and regulations.

The OSHA staff is authorized to conduct investigations and inspections to ensure compliance by employers with the agency's rules and regulations on workers' safety and health.[7] The OSHA investigators are authorized to issue citations to any employer found to be in noncompliance. These activities, however, have made the agency the target of attack from the business community; efforts have been made to curtail its regulatory activities. The agency's powers, however, have been greatly exaggerated; it barks more than it bites.

Mine and Health Administration (MHA)

The MHA is responsible for ensuring compliance by the mining industry with DOL mine safety and health regulations.[8] In order to ensure compliance, the agency is authorized to do the following.

Develop and promulgate mandatory mine safety and health regulations

Assess civil penalties against employers for noncompliance

Conduct investigations

Assist the states in developing mine safety and health programs

Refer criminal violations to the DOJ for prosecution

Coordinate its efforts with the other federal agencies

Employment Standards Administration (ESA)

This agency is primarily responsible for administering DOL programs that deal with the following.

Minimum wages

Overtime standards

Age and sex discrimination

Registration of farm labor contractors

Affirmative action for women, minorities, and handicapped workers on federal contracts and subcontracts

Determination of prevailing wages to be paid on federal contracts

The ESA is divided into three divisions. These play an important part in ensuring that the agency will meet its delegated responsibilities.

1. The Wage and Hour Division (WHD) seeks to ensure compliance by employers with the minimum-wage provisions under the Fair Labor Standards Act (FLSA). The WHD is further authorized to take legal action against any employer who forces his employees to work overtime in violation of the FLSA. This division enforces the Equal Pay Act and the Age Discrimination in Employment Act. The WHD is also authorized to determine the wage rates under the Service Contract Act; Davis–Bacon Act; Public Contracts Act; and Contract and Work Hours and Safety Standards Act.

2. The Office of Workers Compensation Programs (OWCP) is responsible for the administration of the Federal Employees' Compensation Act,[9] the Longshoremen's and Harbor Workers Compensation Act,[10] and the Black Lung Benefits Act.[11]

3. The Office of Federal Contract Compliance Programs (FCCP) is responsible for ensuring that federal contractors and subcontractors implement affirmative-action programs aimed at women, minorities, and the handicapped. However, the impact of its policies vary with the commitment of the administration in power.

Bureau of Labor Statistics (BLS)

The BLS is the research arm of the DOL. Its primary function is to compile data on many areas of interest to employees and employers, including the following.

Unemployment

Employee compensations

Prices

Productivity of the workforce

Occupational health and safety

Growth of the economy

Unlike many of the other agencies within the DOL umbrella, the BLS has no regulatory or enforcement powers. The data its staff collects is readily available to both the public and private sectors for inspection and review. The BLS publishes its research in several publications such as the:

Consumer Price Index;

Monthly Labor Review;

Wholesale Prices and Price Indexes;

Occupational Outlook Handbook;

Occupational Outlook Quarterly; and

Current Wage Developments.

The DOL is both a regulator and a resource tool; it is authorized to enforce numerous statutes, rules, and regulations. The DOL also collects and disseminates valuable economic data. Both employers and employees are forced to deal with the DOL's bureaucratic maze. How America's workforce functions depends, in part, upon the DOL. For additional information, contact the DOL's Office of Information, Publications and Reports, in Washington.

Notes

1. See, 5 U.S.C. 591 and 611.
2. See, 5 U.S.C. 8108.
3. See, *Code of Federal Regulations,* Title XX, chapter 7, part 801.103.
4. See, Title XXXVIII, chapter 43 of the U.S.C.
5. See, 29 U.S.C. 1001 note.
6. See, Occupational Safety and Health Act (84 Stat. 1590).

7. Inspections by the OSHA staff have been curtailed by the Supreme Court. See, *Marshall* v. *Barlows, Inc.,* 98 S.Ct. 1846 (1978).

8. See, 30 U.S.C. 801.

9. See, also the War Hazards Compensation Act and the War Claims Act.

10. See, also the Defense Base Act, Outer Continental Shelf Land Act, and Nonappropriated Fund Instrumentalities Act.

11. See, the Federal Coal Mine Health and Safety Act of 1969.

16 Interior Has the Resources

An announcement made by the U.S. Department of the Interior (DOI) to speed the sale of offshore oil and gas leases to private companies, brought sharp criticism from the nation's environmental groups. In a separate case, the DOI leased thirty-four tracts off the coast of California and announced it would open up additional federal lands for public use.

The department is responsible for the administration of many of the nation's lands; DOI officials administer more than 500 million acres of federal land. They also exercise trust responsibilities for an additional 50 million acres. The department is responsible for the administration and management of the nation's natural resources, historical areas, and Indian reservations.

The DOI is an important Washington fixture because it exercises great power over the nation's land and water resources. It can be a valuable source of information on our environment. However, the department is also a battleground for competing interests; the outcome of these struggles could have an impact on the nation's future.

Who Does What

The department was established in 1849.[1] It was not long before the department became the custodian of the nation's natural resources. Its duties include:

The safeguarding of mineral, land, and water resources;

Conservation of fish and wildlife;

Maintenance of recreational and historical programs;

Promotion of mine health and safety training;

Assistance to Indian tribes;

Management of the territories;

Management of hydroelectric power systems; and

Efforts to reclaim western arid lands.

Decision making at the DOI rests with its secretary and the various agency and bureau heads. The more important DOI decision makers are as follows.

Secretary

Undersecretary

Assistant Secretary for Energy and Minerals

Assistant Secretary for Fish and Wildlife and Parks

Assistant Secretary for Indian Affairs

Assistant Secretary for Policy, Budget, and Administration

Assistant Secretary for Land and Water Resources

Solicitor

However, the task of carrying out the department's policies and programs rests with its agencies and bureaus; these are the department's frontline troops. Understanding how they operate and what their jurisdictions are, can prove valuable to those members of the public who deal with the DOI. Many of these agencies and bureaus operate in an almost quasi-autonomous manner; this gives their staffs great latitude, and it is their staffs which make the daily decisions at the department.

How the Agencies Function

Within the DOI are several important agencies; you should be aware of their jurisdictions and internal politics. How they function can have a profound impact on the department's policies and programs.

The *Office of Hearings and Appeals (OHA)* is a quasi-judicial body with an Administrative Law Judges division and Price Appeal boards. OHA officials hear appeals from departmental decisions rendered in cases dealing with:

Contract disputes;

Indian probate and administrative matters;

Public and acquired lands;

Submerged offshore lands;

Surface coal-mining control and reclamation;

Claims under the Alaskan Native Claims Settlement act; and

Enforcement of restrictions on importation and transportation of endangered species.

Appeals are forwarded to the Director of OHA who assigns them to the administrative law judges for review. The OHA Director is also authorized to establish ad hoc boards to hear special cases; OHA decisions are final and binding.

The *Office of Minerals Policy and Research Analysis (OMPRA)* is the focal point for the development of minerals policies.[2] This agency is responsible for reviewing mineral research; evaluating mineral programs; and formulating mineral policies.

The *Ocean Mining Administration (OMA)* is responsible for developing programs and policies in the area of ocean mining. The agency also assists other departmental entities in formulating policies that affect:

Resources of the Continental Shelf;

Ocean mining negotiations;

Assessments of ocean resources; and

federal efforts in the area of seabed mineral resources.

The *Office of Water Research and Technology (OWRT)* plays an important part in the DOI's water research efforts; its authority in this area rests on the Water Resources Research Act;[3] and Saline Water Conversion Act.[4] The OWRT also carried out (and funds) extensive research in areas connected with domestic water resource problems; production of usable water from sea water; and water contamination. Much of this data is readily available to the public by contacting the OWRT.

The *Office of the Solicitor (OS)* is the department's legal adviser. The OS is divided into eight regions, and each region is headed by a regional solicitor. The OS is headquartered in Washington and is divided into these six divisions:

1. Division of Energy and Resources
2. Division of Indian Affairs
3. Division of Conservation and Wildlife
4. Division of Surface Mining
5. Division of General Law
6. Division of Adminstration

What the Bureaus Do

Within the DOI are also found several bureaus; these play an important role in the department's daily operations. It will serve you well to understand how they operate, and the scope of their jurisdictions.

The *Bureau of Mines (BOM)* is primarily a fact-finding body.[5] The bureau is, among other things, authorized to:

Assess the nation's mineral resources;

Develop mineral mining technologies;

Collect, review, and publish information on mineral resources; and

Conduct studies related to mine health and safety.

The *Geological Surveys (GS)* is also a fact-finding body;[6] it collects, analyzes, and publishes data dealing with the following:

Geological structure and mineral resources of the national domain[7]

Nation's water resources[8]

Nation's topography and geology

Domestic power resources

Value of leasable minerals

Operation of oil and gas leases on public domain

The GS also performs other tasks which affect the private sector. These include the:

Establishment of rates for the production of oil from the outer Continental Shelf

Publishing of maps of mineral and water deposits on public lands

Carrying out of inspections of public lands

Funding of mineral and energy research programs

Providing of data on the location, character, and distribution of water and mineral resources

Evaluation and study of geothermal resources

Much of this information is readily available to the public upon request; the GS publishes a variety of publications.

The *Fish and Wildlife Service (FWS)*[9] consists of a headquarters office in Washington, and six regional offices. The FWS is responsible for the conservation of wildlife and protection of threatened species. Its responsibilities extend to:

Inland sport fisheries;

Wildlife laboratories and centers; and

Research centers at participating universities

The FWS also conducts wildlife surveys, operates wildlife refuges, and enforces import laws that deal with foreign wildlife.

The *National Park Service (NPS)* is responsible for managing the federal parks, historic sites, and recreational lands.[10]

The *Bureau of Indian Affairs (BIA)* became part of the DOI in 1848.[11] The bureau's principal responsibilities are to:

Assist native Indian and Alsakan tribes in matters of health, welfare, and education; and

Act as a trustee for all Indian lands and resources held by the federal government.

The bureau's relations with the Indian tribes has been traditionally marked by controversy and confrontation. It is a marriage that neither side is happy with.

The *Bureau of Land Management (BLM)* is responsible for the managment of:[12]

450 million acres of public lands (many of these are located in the western states and Alaska); and

63 million acres of land where the mineral rights have been reserved by the federal government.

The bureau is also responsible for managing the nation's waterbeds; geothermal, timber, oil, and gas resources; and endangered animal and plant species.

BLM is authorized to handle the sale of the federal lands it manages to private buyers and local governments. The bureau is also authorized to lease these lands and issue rights-of-way.

The *Bureau of Reclamation (BOR)* is responsible for the reclamation of arid and semiarid lands in some seventeen western states and Hawaii.[13] BOR's basic functions include the following.

Assist state and local governments in developing their water resources

Develop industrial water supplies

Develop hydroelectric power plants

Promote private conservation efforts

Develop guidelines for the regulation of water resources

Fund programs that will maximize water resources

Carry out research

Extend loans that will promote the construction or rehabilitation of irrigation networks

Prepare environmental statements for proposed water-resource projects

The *Office of Surface Mining Reclamation and Enforcement (OSMRE)* primarily functions to regulate coal-mining operations.[14] It does they by establishing minimum standards for the regulation of surface coal mining; and promoting the reclamation of formerly mined areas. The bureau delegates its responsibilities to the following four divisions.

1. Abandoned Mines Division: handles reclamation programs and administers the Abandoned Mine Reclamation Fund.
2. Inspection and Enforcement Division: conducts inspections and enforces the bureau's statndards. The division is also authorized to assess penalties.
3. State and Federal Programs Division: reviews and evaluates local mining programs, and also extends assistance to the states and to small mine operators.
4. Technical Services and Research Division: establishes performance and reclamation standards.

The DOI plays an important role in the management of America's natural resources and is an important source of information. It funds programs and research in these areas. The department is also a regulator; it enacts rules and regulations that can have a significant impact on the public. Its policies and objectives, however, are not constant; they change with the shifts in the nation's political climate. The DOI is often responsive to the needs and pressures of the public.

Notes

1. See, 43 U.S.C. 1451.
2. See, Reorganization Plan No. 3 of 1950 (64 Stat. 1262).

3. See, 42 U.S.C. 1961 et seq.

4. See, 42 U.S.C. 1959 et seq.

5. See, 30 U.S.C. 1, 3, 5, 6, and 7.

6. See, 43 U.S.C. 31.

7. See, 43 U.S.C. 31(b).

8. See, 28 Stat. 398.

9. See, *Code of Federal Regulations,* Title L (50) subchapter A, part 2 (70 Stat. 1199).

10. See, 16 U.S.C. 1.

11. See, 25 U.S.C. 13 and 461 et seq.

12. See, the Federal Land Policy and Management Act (90 Stat. 2743).

13. See, 43 U.S.C. 391 et seq.

14. See, 91 Stat. 445.

17 For Housing and Construction, Call HUD

It may surprise you to know that the biggest real-estate developer and landlord is the federal government. Each year, the government spends billions of dollars on land sales, housing construction, and mortgage and insurance programs; it also administers a multitude of other real-estate assistance programs. The executive department with jurisdiction over these multibillion-dollar annual programs is the Department of Housing and Urban Development (HUD).

How HUD Operates

The department was created in 1965 by the Department of Housing and Urban Development Act;[1] its purpose is to administer and oversee the multitude of federal housing-connected programs that were established after World War II. Theoretically the purpose of these programs is to stimulate the construction and housing industries. HUD employs a number of vehicles to do that; what they are and how they function, is of importance to anyone involved in the housing industry. The men and women who administer the programs are equally important to anyone who deals with HUD. The chief officer is the Secretary of HUD; he is responsible for both the administration and formulation of policy at the department. The second-in-command at HUD is the Undersecretary.

There are several other important officials at HUD. Among these is the Assistant Secretary for Legislation and Intergovernmental Relations; he is responsible for both reviewing and representing HUD's interests and legislative positions before the Congress. He is the department's chief lobbyist and is responsible for coordinating its legislative efforts with the other federal agencies and with private groups.

Another important official at HUD is the Assistant Secretary for Administration, who is responsible for the daily management of HUD. The General Counsel (GC) is the department's chief legal adviser. The Inspector General (IG) also plays an important role; he is charged with safeguarding the department's many programs from fraud, theft, and waste. The IG is authorized to investigate all complaints and allegations of fraud; criminal cases are referred to the Department of Justice for prosecution.

The Assistant Secretary for Fair Housing and Equal Opportunity is the department's chief adviser of civil-rights matters. He also administers HUD's fair-housing programs. His staff reviews the department's programs to ensure that they provide for some minority participation; this office has traditionally been sensitive to political pressure by minority groups.

The department is responsive to cues and pressures from congressional committees and the White House staff. Powerful interests in the real-estate industry also exert influence over many of HUD's policies and decisions. However, you need not be an insider to exert influence over HUD. Understanding how the department works and who its key officials are can prove of value; knowledge can be converted into power.

When dealing with HUD, follow these simple rules.

1. Identify the appropriate HUD division with jurisdiction over your problem or needs.
2. Identify and direct your efforts to the appropriate official within that division who has the power to assist you.
3. Identify congressional sources to whom you can turn for assistance should the need arise.
4. Identify White House staffers who can be of assistance. (These need not be the big chiefs.)
5. Be prepared to take legal action should the need arise.

People often turn to expensive Washington professionals to assist them in their dealings with HUD because they believe the insider has the edge. However by simply making the right telephone call, contacting the right person or bureau, and acting the part of an insider, one can open his own doors. The insider has a role to play, but use his services only when your own efforts prove of no avail.

Programs You Should Know

HUD has a number of bureaus and divisions that provide technical and financial assistance to the private sector. Among these is the Office of Community Planning and Development (OCPD). It provides funds to local governments for the purpose of stimulating and assisting the housing industry. An applicant need only demonstrate that he plans to employ the funds to:

Eliminate deteriorated housing;

Augment housing for the poor; or

Save existing housing.

The Housing Community Development Act of 1974 authorizes HUD to provide funds to cities and counties for the purpose of assisting local projects; the objective is to stimulate local economic growth.[2] Additional legislation, in the form of the Uniform Relocation Assistance and Real Property Acquisition Policies Act of 1970, authorizes the department to assist those persons who have been displaced by federally funded programs.

The OCPD's role is to ensure that local governments comply with the department's rules and regulations. The OCPD can also transfer to local governments places of residence that are unoccupied and in need of repair; these are to be used in HUD-approved urban-homesteading programs.[3]

The Office of Assistant Secretary for Housing (OASH) administers programs to rehabilitate and stimulate the construction of housing. These programs include the following.

Low-income housing program (established under the Housing Act of 1937)

Rent-supplement program (established under Title I of the Housing and Urban Development Act of 1965)

Elderly housing loan program (established under Section 202 or the Housing Act of 1959)

Flood-insurance program [established under sections 201(a) and 202(a) of the Flood Disaster Protection Act of 1973]

Technical and financial assistance program for nonprofit sponsors (funded under Section 106 of the Housing and Urban Development Act of 1968)

Disaster housing program

Private market financing program

The OASH also funds programs aimed at assisting in the purchase of single-family dwellings; rental housing; cooperative housing; condominiums; and mobile homes.

Qualifying for Mortgage Insurance

The department funds several mortgage-insurance programs to assist the private sector. Some of these programs cover the following.

Nursing homes

Housing for the elderly

Intermediate care facilities

Nonprofit hospitals

Medical-group practice facilities

HUD also provides mortgage-insurance and loan programs for mobile-home parks; land development projects; experimental housing projects; and urban-renewal housing.

The department's mortgage-insurance programs are administered by several of its agencies. Each of the following agencies is authorized to provide funds and technical assistance to various sectors of the real-estate industry.

1. Government National Mortgage Association (GNMA): is authorized (under Title III of the National Housing Act) to assist in the financing of federally underwritten mortgages. The GNMA also provides financial assistance for low-income housing.
2. Policy Development and Research Office (PDRO): is authorized under the Housing and Urban Development Act of 1970 to conduct surveys of the housing market. The PDRO also measures changes in that market, and publishes these in its *Annual Housing Survey*.
3. Federal Disaster Assistance Administration (FDAA): administers and coordinates the department's disaster assistance programs. The FDAA also funds its own disaster relief and recovery programs.
4. Office of Neighborhoods, Voluntary Associations, and Consumer Protection (ONVACP): oversees HUD's responsibilities in the consumer area. The ONVACP is authorized to seek compliance with the following departmental concerns.
    a. Mobile-home standards. Under Title VI of the Housing and Community Development Act of 1974, HUD has responsibility for establishing safety standards for the construction, design, and performance of mobile homes.
    b. Interstate land sales. Under the Interstate Land Sales Full Disclosure Act, HUD has responsibility for establishing disclosure requirements for developers of fifty or more lots.
    c. Real-estate settlement procedures. Under the Real Estate Settlement Procedure Act of 1974, HUD requires lenders to provide loan applicants with "good faith estimates" of settlement costs and a description of the settlement process.[4]

    d. Lead-poisoning prevention. The Lead-Based Paint Prevention Act of 1971 authorizes HUD to direct the removal of lead-based paints in federally owned or financed property.

For additional information on any of these HUD programs, contact the department's Office of Public Affairs in Washington.

Other Insurance Programs

HUD offers an assortment of insurance programs. These are largely administered and coordinated by the Federal Insurance Administration (FIA). For additional information on the following programs, contact this administration.

Flood Insurance Program: is available to persons who live in areas with flood, mudslide, and erosion problems.

Flood Disaster Protection Program: provides financial assistance for the construction of housing in flood-threatened localities.

Riot Reimbursement Program: provides insurance for property owners in riot-threatened urban areas. The coverage is available through participating private insurance programs and covers fire, vandalism, and malicious mischief.

Federal Crime Insurance Programs: provides burglary and robbery insurance for businesses in high-crime areas, where such coverage is either difficult or unavailable through private channels.

In addition to its programs, HUD offers a variety of films and publications for public use; these are readily available upon request. For information on any of the HUD programs or services, contact its Office of Procurement and Contract in Washington.

Notes

1. See, 42 U.S.C. 3531–3537.
2. See Title VIII, sec. 119 and 810 of the Housing Community Development Act of 1974.
3. See, Title VIII, sec. 810 of the Housing Community Development Act of 1974.
4. See, 12 U.S.C. 2601.

18 Looking Overseas, It's State

"The fundamental objective of our foreign policy," a former Secretary of State said, "is to assure the international conditions of competition and cooperation which can keep our economy strong." The U.S. Department of State (DOS) does more than formulate and coordinate U.S. foreign policy; it also plays a role in international economic policy. Through many of its offices and programs, both in this country and abroad, it helps promote U.S. exports. When looking overseas, turn to the DOS.

How DOS Operates

The DOS has historically served as the President's chief adviser in matters of foreign policy. Its jurisdiction is broad and encompasses the execution of the nation's foreign policies. The department also studies economic, social, and political developments in specific foreign countries; and it conducts formal exchanges and communications with foreign nations. DOS is responsible for negotiating foreign treaties and agreements; establishing and operating consulates and embassies overseas; and representing U.S. interests in more than fifty international organizations.

The administration and formulation of policy at the DOS is the responsibility of several officials. In part, the influence and power that these individuals exert will depend on their experience, personalities, and ties to the administration in power. However, for any person who travels or does business overseas, the decisions of even the most inept of these officials can sometimes have an impact.

If you are going to deal with the DOS, you should know who its key officers are. The Secretary of State is the President's principal foreign-policy adviser, and the first-ranking member of the cabinet. The secretary is responsible for coordinating and supervising U.S. foreign policy; he is also a member of the National Security Council. The Deputy Secretary is the secretary's principal assistant.

The Undersecretary of Political Affairs has responsibility for coordinating the department's dealings with the other federal agencies. He also plays a role in the formulation and coordination of foreign policy.

The Undersecretary for Security Assistance, Science, and Technology coordinates the Security Assistance Program and also serves as the executive chairman of the Interagency Security Assistance Review Program. He is also responsible for the coordination of the department's scientific and technical programs, whereas the Undersecretary for Economic Affairs coordinates DOS foreign economic and scientific programs.

Another important official is the Deputy Undersecretary for Management; he advises the secretary on administrative matters. There is also an Ambassador-at-Large, who serves at the pleasure of the secretary; and a Counselor who advises the secretary on important foreign policy matters. The latter two officials can be assigned to oversee special negotiations.

Understanding the Bureaus

The department's foreign-affairs activities are largely the province of its specialized *regional bureaus*. These are divided geographically, and include the:

Bureau of African Affairs;

Bureau of European Affairs;

Bureau of East Asian and Pacific Affairs;

Bureau of Inter-American Affairs; and

Bureau of Near Eastern and South Asian Affairs

Each bureau is headed by an Assistant Secretary who keeps the Secretary of State advised on issues, policies, and developments that deal with countries within his bureau's jurisdiction. The assistant secretaries are assisted by bureau directors; these also serve as the department's contacts with its embassies and overseas missions.

The DOS also has *functional bureaus*. Each bureau is headed by an Assistant Secretary and has jurisdiction over specific department programs and activities. The following are among the more important of the functional bureaus.

Bureau of Intelligence and Research (BIR): coordinates and supervises the department's intelligence-gathering programs. The BIR also coordinates DOS intelligence activities with those of the other intelligence agencies.

Bureau of Public Affairs (BPA): serves as the department's public-relations office, and also administers the DOS's Freedom of Information Act program.

Bureau of Politico-Military Affairs (BPMA): supervises and coordinates the department's military assistance, nuclear policy, and arms-control programs.

Bureau of International Organization Affairs (BIOA): coordinates the department's efforts in the United Nations and other international organizations.

Bureau of Oceans and International Environmental and Scientific Affairs (BOIESA): has responsibility for a broad range of foreign-policy issues and programs that deal with such areas as fisheries, environment, population, nuclear technology, space, and transfer of technologies.

Bureau of Consular Affairs (BCA): is responsible for the administration and enforcement of all immigration and nationality laws that fall within the department's jurisdiction.

Bureau of Economic and Business Affairs (BEBA): has responsibility for developing and implementing many of the department's foreign economic and business policies.

Bureau of Legal Adviser (BLA): is the department's principal legal adviser.

Office of the Chief of Protocol (OCP): has jurisdiction over the accreditation of foreign diplomats. It also acts as the department's liaison in ceremonial matters with the foreign-diplomatic community in this country.

Agencies and Programs

Within the DOS are also found several other agencies and programs that are instrumental in the development and implementation of foreign political and economic policies. Among these is the Agency for International Development (AID); it has jurisdiction over all DOS assistance programs to Third World nations. Its authority rests on several statutes and executive orders, including the following.

Foreign Assistance Act of 1961 as amended[1]

Executive Order No. 10973[2]

State Department Delegation of Authority No. 104[3]

Agriculture Trade Development Assistance Act of 1954 as amended[4]

Title XII of the Foreign Assistance Act of 1975

The AID is also responsible for handling and coordinating a number of foreign economic-assistance programs. These fall under one of two categories: developmental assistance programs; or security assistance programs. These programs take one or more of the following forms.

1. Loans
2. Technical cooperation
3. Development grants
4. Supplies and relief
5. Credit guaranty programs
6. Self-help programs
7. Population planning and health
8. Agricultural research

The AID runs many of its programs through organizations that are located in foreign nations where the agency carries out its bilateral economic-assistance programs. The foreign-based organizations take the following forms.

1. AID missions
2. AID offices
3. AID sections of embassy
4. Regional service offices

The Foreign Service (FS) handles the department's daily overseas relations. FS personnel operate out of U.S. embassies, missions, consulates, special and branch offices, and consular agencies.

There are a number of other specialized offices within the department. The following are the better known of these.

Passport Office (within the Bureau of Consular Affairs): handles all requests concerning passports.

Office of Public Programs (within the Bureau of Public Affairs): organizes and sponsors conferences and workshops for businesspeople and professionals who are doing or plan to do business overseas.

Office of Special Consular Services (within the Bureau of Consular Affairs): addresses inquiries dealing with missing persons, emergencies, and deaths, involving U.S. citizens in foreign countries.

Visa Office (within the Bureau of Consular Affairs): handles all questions dealing with the issuance of visas to aliens.

Freedom of Information Staff (within the Bureau of Public Affairs): administers the Freedom of Information Act requests directed at the DOS.

Privacy Staff (within the Foreign Affairs Document and Reference Center): administers Privacy Act requests.

Supply and Transportation Division: handles all contract inquiries addressed to DOS.

Anyone planning to travel or do business overseas would do well to understand the services DOS offers to the public, and how it operates. The DOS can prove of assistance, provided you can find your way through this complex network. For additional information on any of the DOS agencies or programs, contact its Bureau of Public Affairs in Washington.

Notes

1. See, 22 U.S.C. 2381.
2. Of November 3, 1961, as amended.
3. See, 26 F.R. 10608 (Of November 3, 1961, as amended).
4. 7 U.S.C. 1691 et seq.

19 Transportation Means Moving Along

The staff of the Department of Transportation (DOT) has considered the redesigning of auto consoles; one of its agencies, the National Highway Traffic Safety Administration, has weighed the advantages of doing away with rules governing odometers. The staff at the DOT also regulates the use of private boats; it has authority to enforce safety regulations in this area.

The DOT exerts powerful influence over the nation's transportation rules and regulations; it does this through several important regulatory agencies. Its rules and regulations have an impact on the nation's transportation policies, planning, and technological developments; and affect the use and development of our air, land, and water transport.

What DOT Does

The department administers and coordinates the numerous federal transportaion programs, rules, and regulations.[1] Its jurisdiction is broad and extends to every facet of the nation's transportation network. It regulates the following areas of transport.

Urban mass transit

Railroads

Aviation

Highway planning and construction

Use of the waterways

Ports

Highways

Oil and gas pipelines

The department consists of the Secretary's Office and eight regulatory agencies. Each of the agency heads reports directly to the Secretary of DOT; however, the agencies operate in an almost autonomous fashion.

The policies and decision making of these agencies are motivated and propelled by the needs, politics, and momentum of their leadership and staffs; each of these agencies responds to its own centrifugal forces.

Because power at the DOT is highly decentralized, members of the public who deal with the department should concentrate their efforts on the individual agencies. This is not to say, however, that the department's top officials exert little or no influence. It is important that one knows who these officials are, the roles that they play in the DOT's decision-making processes, and the scopes of their power.

The following officials are among the department's more important and powerful decision makers.

1. The Secretary of Transportation: serves as the principal adviser to the President on all federal policies and matters dealing with the nation's transportation systems.[2] Final responsibility for the planning, direction, and administration of the department and its agencies rests with this official.

2. The Deputy Secretary: assists the secretary in running the department; he also acts in the secretary's absence.

3. The Assistant Secretary for Policy and International Affairs: is responsible for the review and development of domestic and international transportation policies. His office funds research in the area of transportation, and provides foreign governments with technical assistance.

4. The Assistant Secretary for Budget and Programs: advises the secretary on budgetary needs and resources. He also periodically evaluates DOT programs, and reviews its legislative needs.

5. The Secretary for Administration: advises the DOT Secretary on matters dealing with the department's internal management.

6. The Secretary for Governmental Affairs: is the department's liaison with Congress, and coordinates all of its lobbying efforts.

7. The General Counsel: is the department's chief legal adviser. His office represents the DOT and its agencies in much of their administrative and civil litigation. He also reviews all pending or proposed legislation that could affect the department's jurisdiction and interests.

8. The Board of Contract Appeals: hears and decides on all appeals from decisions by DOT contract officers.

9. The Secretarial Representative: represents the DOT Secretary in many of the department's dealings with private groups and individuals; initial contacts with the DOT often occur at this level.

The Work of the Agencies

The department's everyday policies and operations are, in most instances, the work of its agencies. These are directly responsible to the Secretary of Transportation, and often operate in a quasi-autonomous fashion. Each agency has its own head and vested interests. Being familiar with the jurisdictions, politics, and operations of the important DOT agencies, can help an outsider deal with the DOT.

The Federal Aviation Administration (FAA)[3] is responsible for issuing and enforcing rules and regulations that deal with air commerce; aviation safety; national system of airports; air-traffic-control systems; and air-navigation systems. In addition, the FAA oversees the:

Manufacture, operation, and maintenance of aircraft;

Certification of airports serving air carriers; and

Inspection of air-navigation facilities.

The FAA is also responsible for the registration of private aircraft, their engines and propellers; and the recording of their ownership. The agency is responsible for such other tasks as:

Allocating the use of airspace;

Administering aviation war risk insurance; and

Administering aircraft war loan-guaranty programs

The Federal Railroad Administration (FRA) is responsible for the administration and enforcement of the federal rail safety laws and regulations.[4] It is authorized by the Rail Safety Act of 1970 to administer and enforce safety regulations that deal with locomotives, signals, power brakes, and railroad accidents.

The FRA also administers assistance programs directed at local and federal rail services. Under the Railroad Revitalization and Regulatory Reform Act of 1976, the agency is authorized to promote and assist minority-owned businesses.

The Maritime Administration (MA) provides subsidies and incentives to the domestic merchant fleet through the Maritime Subsidiary Board. The MA is also authorized to guarantee the construction, reconstruction, and reconditioning of domestic carrier vessels. In addition, it insures operators and seamen (when domestic insurance is not available) against losses caused by hostile action. The MA administers grant programs for the private maritime academies, and operates the U.S. Merchant Marine Academy.

The Urban Mass Transportation Administration (UMTA) operates under the authority of the Urban Mass Transportation Act of 1964.[5] The UMTA is authorized to encourage and assist urban mass-transportation systems. It also provides financial assistance to both public and private groups involved in mass-transit projects.

The National Highway Traffic Safety Administration (NHTSA)[6] has jurisdiction over federal programs that deal with the safety and performance of motor vehicles, equipment, drivers, and pedestrians.[7] The NHTSA is also responsible for enforcing rules and regulations under the following statutes.

1. National Traffic and Motor Vehicle Safety Act of 1966[8]
2. Motor Vehicle Information and Cost Saving Act[9]
3. Clean Air Amendments of 1970[10]

In addition, the NHTSA administers federal laws and regulations that deal with:

Odometers;

Speed limits;

Fuel-economy standards;

Traffic-safety programs;

Research and development programs; and

Registration of revoked operator's licenses.

The Federal Highway Administration (FHA) is authorized under the Department of Transportation Act to administer the department's various highway transportation programs.[11] The agency also administers programs that deal with the following matters.

Financial assistance for state highway construction

Improvements of highway safety

Safety standards in highway design, construction, and maintenance

The FHA exercises regulatory jurisdiction over the safety and performance of commercial motor carriers engaged in interstate commerce. Its staff is authorized to investigate commerce. Its staff is authorized to investigate (and refer to the Department of Justice for criminal prosecution) cases that involve violations of the following.

1. Highway Safety Act
2. Interstate Commerce Act
3. Explosives and Dangerous Articles Act
4. Federal Motor Carrier Safety Regulations
5. Hazardous Materials Transportation Regulations

The Coast Guard (CG) is one of the oldest and best known of the federal agencies. Its primary function is that of a regulator.[12] The regulations it enforces are broad and encompass the following.

Safety standards for commercial vessels

Offshore structures on the outer Continental Shelf

Investigations of marine-related accidents, casualties, and violations

Pilotage services on the Great Lakes

Security and safety of ports

Aids to navigation systems

Construction, maintenance, and operation of bridges across navigable waters

All proposed CG regulations are first considered and reviewed by the Marine Safety Council.

The Research and Special Programs Administration (RSPA) is responsible for carrying out and enforcing DOT responsibilities that relate to pipeline safety and security; and transportation of hazardous cargo. Much of the RSPA's daily work is carried out by its bureaus. The more important of these are the Materials Transportation Bureau; Transportation Systems Center; and Transportation Programs Bureau.

From the time you enter your automobile, DOT rules and regulations dictate what and how you drive, the types of roads on which you drive, the speed at which you drive, and even the tires on which you drive. The auto manufacturers, commercial carriers, and others in related industries, are regulated daily by one or more of the department's agencies. For additional information on the DOT, contact its Office of Public and Consumer Affairs in Washington.

Notes

1. See, 49 U.S.C. 1651 note.
2. See, *Code of Federal Regulations,* Title XLIX, part I, subject B, for additional information on the powers of this official.
3. See, the *Federal Register,* volume 30, page 3395, as amended at 30 F.R. 8728 and 31 F.R. 838.
4. See, section 3(e)(1) of the Department of Transportation Act of 1966 (80 Stat. 932).
5. See, 49 U.S.C. 1601 et seq.

6. For additional information, see the *Code of Federal Regulations,* Title XLIX, part 501.

7. See, Highway Safety Act of 1970, 84 Stat. 1739.

8. See, 80 Stat. 718.

9. See, 86 Stat. 947.

10. See, 86 Stat. 1700.

11. See, 80 Stat. 932.

12. See, 14 U.S.C. 1.

20 Treasury Is Where the Bucks Are

A New Jersey dentist who had failed to file a tax return for two consecutive years, was indicted and pleaded guilty to tax fraud. In Texas, a bank employee was arrested by the U.S. Secret Service and charged with the theft of federal funds. He had been implicated in a multimillion-dollar rip-off of a federal agency. In New York, U.S. Customs Service agents interdicted a shipment of stolen artifacts.

The Department of the Treasury is not just the nation's banker; it houses more than a dozen important agencies such as the Internal Revenue Service (IRS), the Office of the Comptroller of the Currency, and the U.S. Customs Service. These agencies have important law-enforcement and regulatory functions at the national level.

Who Rolls the Coins

The agencies, bureaus, and divisions of the Treasury Department each have their own statutory turf and constituency. They perform, in varying degrees, one or more of the following basic functions.

1. Enforcing the law
2. Manufacturing currency
3. Serving as the federal government's financial agent
4. Recommending and formulating tax and fiscal policies

The Treasury affects all facets of our financial sector. How decisions are made at the department depends upon its key officials; they are the men and women who roll the coins. Chief among them is the Treasury Secretary. He advises the President on a broad range of fiscal policies and the public debt. As chief financial officer of the federal government, he also chairs the Economic Policy Group; governs the International Monetary Fund; and represents the United States in the African Development Fund, the Inter-American Development Bank, and the International Bank for Reconstruction and Development.

The secretary is also responsible for seeing that the department carries out its law-enforcement functions. The Deputy Secretary acts as the secretary's representative in his absence.

The Treasury is a complex department with many officials in charge of specific duties. The more important assistants to the Treasury Secretary include the following.

Undersecretary

Undersecretary for Monetary Affairs

Assistant Secretaries for:

   Domestic Affairs

   International Affairs

   Public Affairs

   Legislative Affairs

   Enforcement and Operations

   Administration

   Economic Policy

Office of Fiscal Assistant Secretary

Office of General Counsel

Office of the Director of Practice

Office of Assistant Secretary for Tax Policy

How the Agencies Function

There are several important bureaus within the Treasury Department that play an important role in carrying out the department's statutory responsibilities. Understanding how these agencies function will help anyone who deals with the Treasury.

Office of the Comptroller of the Currency (OCC)

The OCC is an integral part of the national banking system[1] The comptroller is responsible for the following.[2]

   Administration of federal laws that deal with the national banks

   Regulation of the national banks

Enactment of rules and regulations dealing with national banks

Conversion of state chartered banks into national banks

Bank mergers that result in a national bank

Establishment of national bank branches

Internal Revenue Service (IRS)

The IRS is primarily responsible for administering and enforcing the internal-revenue laws, and other tax-related functions.[3] The IRS is one of the more important and complex of the departmental agencies. Its key organizational components are its National Office; regional offices; district offices; and service centers.

The IRS headquarters, or National Office, is located in Washington, D.C. This office is responsible for developing the agency's national policies. There are seven regional offices; each is headed by a commissioner. These offices hear disputes from and supervise the district offices.

At the local level are found the IRS district offices. Each office has jurisdiction over several counties within a state, and is headed by a director. The district offices are responsible for the following functions.

Determining tax liabilities

Conducting audits of tax returns

Holding conferences on disputed liabilities

Determining pension-plan qualifications

Collecting delinquent taxes

Investigating criminal and civil violations of the tax code

Initially processing applications to practice before the IRS.

There are also IRS service centers, which fall under the supervision of the regional commissioners. They carry out the following duties.

Processing tax returns

Maintaining records of taxes collected

Administering assigned audits

Overseeing investigative functions

Audit procedures. Of greatest concern to the public is the dreaded IRS audit. Audits are guided by rules and regulations; understanding these should help you stave off or survive an audit. The IRS employs the following guidelines (as deatiled in section 100 of the Internal Revenue Service's Law Enforcement Manual IX) to prosecute tax-related criminal violations.[4]

1. Criminal prosecution will be recommended in a case where the average yearly additional tax is $2,500 or more, and which utilizes the specific-item method of proof and involves uncomplicated fact patterns.
2. Prosecution will be recommended in a case that utilizes an indirect method of proof or involves complex tax-evasion schemes, and where the additional tax totals at least $10,000 for the prosecution period and the additional tax for any single year within that period is at least $3,000.
3. Criminal prosecution will be recommended in any altered-document case if the additional tax is $500 or more for any year in question.
4. Investigative preference will be given to those cases that span three prosecution years rather than cases involving violations provable as to only one or two years.
5. Criminal prosecution may be recommended in cases where flagrant or repetitious conduct makes resort to criminal sanctions necessary; for example where:
   a. The taxpayer has persisted in attempting to mislead the IRS or has concealed fraudulent schemes.
   b. The case involves a scheme known to be in frequent use by other taxpayers and this widespread use is believed to have a serious adverse affect on voluntary compliance.
   c. The facts and circumstances are so flagrant as to warrant the conclusion that a reasonable probability of conviction exists.

There are several points that one should be aware of when dealing with an IRS audit. The first indication of an audit will be a notification letter. During the audit procedures one can be represented by either counsel or the preparer of his return. Any communications regarding the audit should be limited only to the matters raised by the examiner; past returns should not be discussed nor information about them volunteered.

Audits can be conducted within three years from the filing deadline. If a taxpayer has omitted from his return income in excess of 25 percent, the IRS has up to six years from the filing deadline to conduct an audit. However, if a taxpayer has not filed a return, there is no deadline for conducting an audit; and there is no deadline in cases of criminal fraud.

Court procedures. If you are audited and are unhappy with the examiner's decision, you can appeal it to the examiner's immediate supervisor, or through the IRS Appeals Office. You can also skip the IRS internal procedures altogether and go directly to court.[5] Before you decide to opt for the courts, consider the following information.

The Tax Court will hear your dispute before you have paid the disputed sum to the IRS.

A U.S. district court and the U.S. Court of Claims will require that you first pay the taxes in question and then file with the IRS for a refund. If the refund request is rejected, then you can file a lawsuit in any of these courts.

The Tax Court will handle small disputes of up to $5,000 for any one year. The following are added advantages in dealing with the Tax Court.

1. Its procedures and rules of evidence are less formal than those of a U.S. district court
2. A petition can be filed within ninety days of deficiency notice
3. A decision cannot be appealed by either side
4. It holds sessions in more than one hundred cities

Customs Service (CS)

The CS plays an important role in collecting revenue from imports and enforcing customs-related laws, rules, and regulations. It administers the Tariff Act of 1930,[6] and assesses and collects customs duties, excise taxes, fees, and penalties. The CS can seize contraband; and process traffic (in and out of the country) of persons, mail, carriers, and cargo. The CS can also prosecute evasions of customs laws and enforce the Antidumping Act.

The CS is responsible for enforcing more than 400 rules and regulations in areas that impact on international trade; including copyrights, patents, countervailing duty, trademarks, and quotas. The CS has its headquarters in Washington and is headed by the Commissioner of Customs. The CS is divided into nine regions, forty-five area offices, and three hundred ports of entry; it has field offices in nine foreign cities.

The Customs Service also shares responsibility with other federal agencies in enforcing the following.

Automobile safety and emission standards[7]

Prohibitions against the discharge of refuse and oil into the coastal waters[8]

Standards for radioactive materials

Counterfeiting statutes dealing with monetary instruments

Flammable-fabric restrictions

Animal and plant quarantines

Hazardous-substance prohibitions

The CS also assists businesses engaged in international trade. For additional information on the CS, contact the Special Assistant to the Commissioner, U.S. Customs Service, Washington, D.C.

The Other Treasury Agencies and Their Responsibilities

1. U.S. Secret Service: is responsible for safeguarding the following personages.
   a. President and his immediate family
   b. President Elect
   c. Vice-President and his immediate family
   d. Vice-President Elect
   e. Former Presidents and their wives and widows
   f. Visiting heads of state
2. Bureau of the Mint: is responsible for the following.[10]
   a. Production of coinage
   b. Distribtuion of coins to Federal Reserve Banks
   c. Custody, processing, and movement of bullion
   d. Compilation and review of worldwide data on gold and silver
3. Bureau of the Public Debt: is responsible for the following.
   a. Establishing regulations for federal-government securities
   b. Regulating audits of retired securities and interest coupons
   c. Conducting transactions in outstanding securities
   d. Overseeing the public debt and expenditures
   e. adjudicating claims arising from securities that are lost, mutilated, stolen, or destroyed
4. U.S. Savings Bonds Divison: has jurisdiction and responsibility for promoting and regulating the sale of savings bonds.
5. Bureau of Engraving and Printing (BEP): is responsible for the U.S. production of the following.[11]

a. Paper currency
b. Bonds
c. Bills
d. Notes
e. Certificates
f. Postage stamps
g. Customs stamps

6. Bureau of Government Financial Operations (BGFO): is charged with the following departmental fiscal responsibilities.

   a. Accounting, reporting, and disclosure of U.S. Treasury assets and liabilities
   b. Reporting on the financial status and operations of the federal government
   c. Issuance of payments to beneficiaries of federal benefit programs
   d. Foreign disbursements
   e. Adjudication of claims arising from Treasury checks that are lost, stolen, or forged
   f. Supervision of federal grant-in-aid programs
   g. Supervision of the federal government's depository system
   h. Handling of claims arising out of destroyed currency
   i. Regulation of surety companies on federal bonds
   j. Administration of international claims and judgements
   k. Billing and collecting of funds due by foreign governments

7. Federal Law Enforcement Training Center (FLETC):[12] serves as a training center for more than thirty federal law-enforcement agencies (located in Glynco, Georgia).

Treasury has broad jurisdiction over a number of important sectors of the economy. Companies doing business either domestically or overseas should be aware of its operations. The department is responsible for important regulatory and law-enforcement functions. Its many bureaus and agencies affect our lives daily. Professionals and nonprofessionals alike would benefit by understanding the department's workings. For additional information on the department or any of its agencies, contact its Office of Public Affairs in Washington.

Notes

1. See, *Code of Federal Regulations*, Title XII, part 4.
2. See, 12 Stat. 665.
3. See, 26 U.S.C. 3900.
4. IRS criminal prosecutions are brought under sections 7201, 7206, and 7207 of the Federal Internal Revenue Code.
5. See, IRS Publication No. 556 for information on appeals.

6. See, 19 U.S.C. 1202.

7. As required by the National Traffic and Motor Vehicle Safety Act of 1966 and the Clean Air Act.

8. See, the Oil Pollution Act.

9. See, 18 U.S.C. 508, 509, and 871.

10. See, 1 Stat. 246, and 31 U.S.C. 251–287.

11. See, 31 U.S.C. 171, 181(a), and 415.

12. See, Treasury Department Order No. 217.

Part III
The Independent Regulators

21 The Public Watchdogs

A California man is said to have operated a major commodity trading fraud which bilked several hundred investors out of millions of dollars. It is alleged that he misled the investors by falsely representing that he could double their money in a short span of time. In a separate case, the Federal Trade Commission sought to approve a highly controversial pro-consumer regulation; industry lobbyists were hard at work trying to derail it. Residents of a small township in New Jersey sought federal assistance against a chemical-disposal company; they charged that the company had improperly handled toxic wastes.

In a complex society such as ours, consumers look to Washington for assistance. Our economy is regulated; and with regulation, also come responsibilities and obligations. Congress created the public watchdogs to ensure compliance. How they operate and what their jurisdictions and powers are, is the concern of this chapter.

Federal Trade Commission (FTC)

One of the best known of the public watchdogs, the FTC was organized as an independent agency pursuant to the Federal Trade Commission Act.[1] Additional duties were delegated to the agency by the following acts.

1. Wheeler–Lea Act
2. Trans-Alaska Pipeline Authorization Act
3. Clayton Antitrust Act
4. Export Trade Act
5. Wool Products Labeling Act
6. Fur Products Labeling Act
7. Textile Fiber Products Identification Act
8. Fair Packaging and Labeling Act
9. Robinson–Patman Act
10. Lanhem Trademark Act
11. Truth-in-Lending Act
12. Fair Credit Reporting Act

13. Magnuson–Moss Warranty—Federal Trade Commission Improvement Act

The FTC is composed of five commissioners; these are nominated by the President and confirmed by the Senate for seven-year terms. No more than three of the commissioners may be members of the same party. The agency has a broad mandate and its rules and regulations affect almost every business that engages in interstate or foreign commerce.

During the 1950s, the FTC appeared to consumer groups to favor the corporate world. It was not until the mid-1960s that the agency embarked on a more consumer-directed strategy; in the 1970s it became one of Washington's more important and aggressive regulatory bodies. Although its policies are effected by those who head it, the FTC continues to evoke concern in the business camp.

The agency's basic function is to ensure that competition continues to prevail in our economy. Its basic role can be summarized as preventing and deterring the use in interstate or foreign commerce of unfair methods of competition, and unfair or deceptive acts or practices.

Price-fixing agreements, boycotts, illegal combinations of competitors, and other business practices that hinder competition are illegal under the agency's rules and regulations, and its legislative mandate. Further, the dissemination of false or deceptive advertisement in the areas of consumer products, food, drugs, and cosmetics is prohibited.

The FTC's policing powers are broad and affect the following.

Price discriminations

Exclusive-dealing and tying arrangements

Corporate mergers, acquisitions, and joint ventures (if their result is to lessen competition)

Discrimination among competing customers in the furnishing of payments for services, or facilities for the purpose of promoting the resale of products

The agency is also authorized to protect the consuming public against the circulation of inaccurate or obsolete credit reports, and to ensure that consumer reporting agencies comply with federal law.[2]

The FTC has authority to ensure that retailers, finance companies, nonfederal credit unions, and other creditors make accurate credit disclosure.[3] It also regulates the packaging and labeling of specific consumer commodities, for the purpose of preventing consumer deception.[4]

The FTC has broad enforcement powers. These are of a civil and administrative nature and fall under one of two headings:

1. Actions that encourage voluntary compliance; or
2. Actions that culminate in some court order directed at the offender.

Voluntary-compliance action often takes the form of advisory opinions, issuance of guidelines, and trade regulation rules. Representations by the staff are not binding on the FTC. Policy and rule making rest with the five commissioners; the staff simply acts in their name. All power stems from the five-member ruling body.

FTC administrative actions are analogous to court proceedings. A complaint is issued; in it the staff delineates the charges or offenses alleged. These involve alleged violations of one or more of the rules, regulations, or laws that the FTC administers.

Not all FTC administrative actions culminate in a formal hearing. Many of these are settled through consent orders and other informal channels. If a formal hearing is held, and an FTC administrative law judge finds merit in the staff's charges, an order to cease and desist will be issued directing the offender (known as a respondent) to cease the unlawful activity. The respondent can be a person, partnership, or an organization.

Allegations of unlawful activity can come to the agency's attention from numerous sources. The more common are:

Congressional committees, members, or staffers.

The staff of another government agency (federal, state, or local).

A member of the public.

A competitor of the offender.

The agency's staff (from an informal inquiry).

Consumer groups.

The news media (newspaper articles or reports, TV or radio commentaries).

Complaints addressed to the FTC need not be formal. A letter detailing the alleged violations often suffices. The agency will not (as a matter of policy) disclose the identity of the complainant. (The FOIA can be employed to obtain this information on occasion.) The complaint will often include supporting documents and other evidence. Most complaints, however, go unanswered. Red tape, bureaucratic ineptitude, limited resources, and the agency's priorities, all affect the staff's decision.

However, if an investigation is initiated, at its completion the staff can make one of the following recommendations.

That the case be closed

That an informal settlement be ratified

That a formal complaint be issued

If the majority of the commissioners opts for the latter route, the offender is served with a copy of the staff's complaint and proposed order. Prior to the administrative hearing, however, counsel for the offender will often negotiate some sort of settlement with the staff. The agreement is known as a *consent order*. If no such agreement should result, a formal triallike hearing will follow.

FTC administrative hearings are public and result in a written decision. The decision becomes final at the end of thirty days; the respondent can appeal the decision within this period of time to the commission. The commission then has several options; it can modify, reverse, or sustain the administrative law judge's order. If the respondent disagrees with the commission's decision, he can appeal it to the appropriate U.S. court of appeals. The latter in turn can affirm, modify, or set it aside.

Violations of final FTC orders can result in fines of up to $10,000 per violation. In the case of a continuing violation, each separate day of its continuance constitutes a separate offense. The commission is authorized to issue administrative subpoenas. After consulting with the Department of Justice, it can file suit in federal court to enforce compliance. It can enjoin actions that it deems to be harmful to the public interest (provided an appropriate statute applies).

The agency often conducts studies on diverse economic conditions and problems that may affect competition. These studies sometimes become the basis for some form of congressional action, or industrywide voluntary change.

The FTC publishes quarterly reports on the financial status of the nation's manufacturing industries. These are classified by industry and size. The agency is an important component in the federal regulatory scheme. For additional information on the agency, contact its Office of Public Information in Washington.

Federal Communications Commission (FCC)

The FCC was created under the Communications Act of 1934, for the purpose of regulating interstate and foreign wire and radio communications.[5] With the growth of the broadcasting industry, the FCC has become one of Washington's more important agencies; like many of the other federal regulators, it has become the private preserve of those it regulates.

The scope of the FCC's jurisdiction encompasses any and all interstate or foreign communications involving:

Radio and television broadcasting.

Telephone and telegraph operations.

Cable-television operations.

Two-way radio transmissions.

Radio operators.

Satellite communications.

The agency also performs the following functions.

Licenses and regulates stations and operators

Allocates bands of frequencies to private services

Regulates common carriers

Assigns frequencies to individual stations

Power at the FCC is vested in a seven-member commission. Each member serves a seven-year term. The commissioners are nominated by the President and confirmed by the Senate; the chairperson of the commission is designated by the President. No more than four of these individuals may be members of the same political party.

The commission is assisted by a General Counsel; the latter has exclusive control of all court appeals involving broadcasting matters. There is also a Review Board which is responsible for reviewing initial agency decisions; the board is also responsible for writing the commission's decisions. The FCC has an Administrative Law Judges section which conducts all of the agency's adjudicatory hearings and renders written decisions.

Much of the FCC's investigation and enforcement responsibilities are carried out by its Field Operations Bureau (FOB). The bureau has more than two dozen field offices that enforce the agency's rules and regulations. The FOB is also responsible for maintaining field monitoring stations; their function is to detect unlicensed activity.

The Broadcast Bureau (BB) is responsible for the administration of the agency's regulatory program involving:

Radio (AM and FM), television, international shortwave, and connected auxiliary services.

The issuance of construction permits, operating licenses, and renewals or transfers of licenses.

The Safety and Special Radio Services Bureau (SRSB) has responsibility for administering regulations dealing with a broad range of radio services, including the following.

Amateur

Marine

Aviation

Public safety

Industrial

Transportation

Signaling

Control

Citizen

The SRSB also enforces provisions of treaties dealing with the use of radio communications at sea.

The Common Carrier Bureau (CCB) administers all FCC regulatory programs dealing with interstate and foreign communications by telephone, telegraph, radio, and satellite. The CCB's jurisdiction extends to all companies, organizations, and persons that provide communications service for hire. This includes common carriers that make use of wire or cable facilities, land mobile radios, point-to-point microwave, and satellite systems.

The Cable Television Bureau (CTB) is responsible for administering the FCC's cable-television programs. It has authority to issue certificates of compliance, and to coordinate its efforts with state and local regulators. Cable-television operators are required by the FCC to obtain a certificate of compliance before commencing any operations, or adding additional broadcast signals to their existing operations.

With the growth of the computer and telecommunications revolution, the FCC's jurisdiction appears to be increasing. The agency, however, has also had its problems with sister federal agencies as regards computer and telecommunications services. For example, rivalry has ensued with the U.S. Postal Service over the regulation of the new electronic message systems. Disputes may also arise over the regulation of electronic funds-transfer systems and the electronic newspaper. For additional information on the agency, contact its Public Information Office in Washington.

Environmental Protection Agency (EPA)

The EPA is an independent regulatory agency of the executive branch.[6] Final authority rests with an administrator, who in turn is assisted by six assistant administrators; these seven officials are nominated by the President and confirmed by the Senate. The EPA's function is to protect our environment from misuse and abuse; and specifically to control various types of pollution.

The EPA is also responsible for coordinating and funding the research and antipollution efforts of state and local governments, private and public groups, individuals, and educational institutions. It is empowered to review the potential impact federal projects and policies may have on the environment. The agency publishes its findings; especially if a determination is made that a project or policy may adversely affect the public's health and welfare. Needless to say, defining a healthy environment is not always an easy task; thus, EPA has become a battleground for various competing interests.

The agency's basic activities fall under five broad categories. These are as follows.

1. *Enforcement.* Enforcement is handled by the Office of the Assistant Administrator of Enforcement. Activities in this area involve violations of the agency's air, water, solid waste, toxic substance, radiation, and noise control programs.

2. *Toxic Substances.* Programs in this area are the province of the Office of Assistant Administrator for Toxic Substances. These include guidelines for: assessing chemical substances; rules and regulations for industry; impact evaluations for new chemicals; establishment of standards for the testing of chemicals; and development of appropriate controls. Additional activities include the control and regulation of pesticides, and enactment of tolerance levels for chemicals found in food. Programs in this area include the investigation of pesticide accidents; and the monitoring of pesticide residue levels in food, fish, wildlife, and humans.

3. *Air and Waste Management.* The EPA is responsible for developing national standards, policies, and regulations in the area of air-pollution control. One of its responsibilities in this area is to develop national emission standards for hazardous pollutants.

4. *Water and Hazardous Material.* The function of these EPA programs is to develop national policies and regulations in the area of water-

pollution control. These programs also assist in the development of regional water policies and regulations.

5. *Research and Development.* This is the responsibility of the EPA's Office of the Assistant Administrator for Research and Development. This office is responsible for overseeing research activities carried out by the EPA's national laboratories, and also for coordinating research efforts with state and local government regulatory bodies.

The agency's delegated tasks are often carried out by its ten regional offices. Each of these is headed by a regional administrator, who is responsible for ensuring that the EPA's programs are carried out within the region. For additional information on the agency, contact its Public Information Center in Washington.

Commodity Futures Trading Commission (CFTC)

The CFTC was established as an independent agency under the Commodity Futures Trading Act of 1974.[7] Its function is to regulate trade in agricultural and other commodities transacted in the commodity exchanges. It also has jurisdiction over trading in lumber and metals.

Policy and rule making within the CFTC rests with a five-member commission. The members of the commission serve seven-year terms, and are appointed by the President with the advice of the Senate. The commission's chairperson is designated by the President; no more than three of its members may belong to the same party. Complaints of fraud, price manipulations, and other abuses are the province of its enforcement unit.

The CFTC's responsibilities, however, extend beyond the regulation of the commodity-futures market. It is also responsible for deterring and prosecuting:

Abuses involving commodity trades.

Price manipulations.

The cornering of markets.

The dissemination of false and misleading information that could impact on the price of commodities.

Frauds that involve the handling of traders' funds.

The misuse of customer funds.

The Commodity Futures Trading Act authorizes the agency to:

Promulgate rules and regulations for the commodity-futures market.

Provide for the registration of persons involved in futures trading; for example, commodity trading advisers and pool operators.

Regulate option transactions in commodities.

Regulate leverage contracts in silver and gold.

Require contract markets to provide settlement procedures for customer-related claims and grievances.

Enjoin conduct that is in violation of the act.

Impose fines and penalties for violations of the act.

Prosecute its own civil cases.

The CFTC has been called a paper tiger by its critics. Critics also charge that the agency's legislative mandate is fraught with legal loopholes; its record, they note, has been mediocre at best. The outcome of this debate may yet decide the agency's future; at present, however, it is the federal cop on the commodity beat. For additional information on the CFTC, contact its Office of Public Affairs in Washington.

Consumer Product Safety Commission (CPSC)

The CPSC was established in 1972 as an independent agency.[8] Decision making at the CPSC, and the formulation of policy, rests with its five-member commission. These individuals are appointed by the President, with the consent of the Senate; their terms of service run for seven years. No more than three of these members can come from the same political party; the agency's chairperson is designated by the President.

The congressional intent in creating the CPSC was to:

Safeguard the public from unreasonable risk of injury from consumer products. (For example, it can prohibit the transportation of refrigerators that do not have door safety devices.)

Assist the public in evaluating the safety of consumer products.

Ban hazardous consumer products.

Enact uniform safety standards for consumer products.

Establish mandatory product safety.

Promote research in the area of consumer-product safety.

Investigate injuries, deaths, or illnesses connected to consumer products.

The agency is also responsible for administering the following acts.

1. Poison Prevention Packaging Act[9]
2. Flammable Fabrics Act[10]
3. Hazardous Substances Act[11]

Interested persons, including consumer groups, are authorized to petition the CPSC to issue, amend, or revoke any of its rules dealing with consumer-product safety. The agency's enforcement program, however, has come under sttack. Consumers charge that it is probusiness; business charges that the agency's rules and regulations are costly. The debate rages. For additional information, contact its Office of Public Affairs in Washington.

Equal Employment Opportunity Commission (EEOC)

The EEOC was created under Title VII of the Civil Rights Act of 1964.[12] The EEOC is an independent agency; decision making rests with five commissioners. These are nominated by the President and confirmed by the Senate for five-year terms; the President designates the chairperson.

The EEOC has regional and district offices. It can hear complaints of discrimination against both public and private employers; cases are handled by its field offices. The EEOC staff, however, can also initiate its own investigations. All Title VII charges must be filed with the agency within 180 days of the alleged violation. If the charges were initially filed with a state or local fair-employment-practices agency, the period is extended to 300 days.

Once a charge is filed with the EEOC, its staff has up to ten days to notify the person(s) charged. Charges are often deferred for sixty days to an appropriate local agency; sometimes the EEOC will proceed with its own investigation before the expiration of this period. During this period, the agency's staff will attempt to encourage the parties in dispute to settle informally prior to a determination by its staff. Fact-finding conferences are used to assist in a negotiated settlement.

Even when the staff concludes its investigation and determines that the charges are correct, it will continue to make an effort (through conciliation or persuasion) to have the parties resolve their dispute informally. However, should these efforts fail, the staff may recommend to its commission civil action 30 days after the charges are filed. If a state or local government agency is involved, only the U.S. Attorney General can bring the lawsuit. In the event that the EEOC or the Attorney General fail to bring an action, the agency will then issue a Notice of Right to Sue. This authorizes the aggrieved party to proceed (within 90 days) with its own civil action.

The EEOC, however, can intervene where private actions are of general public interest. In these cases, the agency's staff concludes that prompt judicial action is warranted. Thus, it can recommend to the commission an action for appropriate temporary relief pending a final disposition of the case.

The EEOC also issues guidelines regarding discrimination in employment. It maintains direct liaison with state and local governments, labor and trade groups, civil-rights groups, and other federal agencies concerned with employment discrimination.

The EEOC also publishes data on the employment status of minorities and women. This information is shared with public and private sources. The effectiveness of the agency has been challenged on occasion; it has both supporters and detractors. Its future, however, remains safe. For additional information on the EEOC, contact its Office of Public Affairs, Washington, D.C.

The policies and enforcement tactics of the independent regulators will often depend on the administration in power and the heads of the commissions. Members of the public would do well to better understand these federal watchdogs because of the important impact they can have on our economy and general well-being.

Notes

1. See, 15 U.S.C. 41–51.
2. See, the Fair Credit Reporting Act.
3. See, Truth-in-Lending Act.
4. See, Fair Packaging and Labeling Act.
5. See, 15 U.S.C. 21, and 47 U.S.C. 35, 151–609. See also, 47 U.S.C. 701–744.
6. See, Reorganization Plan No. 3 of 1970.
7. See, 7 U.S.C. 4a; also see, *Code of Federal Regulations*, Title XVII, part 140.
8. See, 86 Stat. 1207.
9. See, 84 Stat. 1670.
10. See, 15 U.S.C. 1191.
11. See, 15 U.S.C. 1261.
12. See, 42 U.S.C. 2000a.

Appendix 21A
Handling EEO Litigation

Procedures in an EEO Hearing

The following procedures are followed in an EEO hearing.

1. The complainant is given an opportunity to present his case first.
2. The following individuals will be permitted in the hearing room:
   a. Complaints examiner
   b. Official recorder
   c. Complainant
   d. Complainant's representative
   e. Agency representative
   f. Witness
3. Each party may make an opening statement on what he intends to prove.
4. Each party will be afforded an opportunity to examine and cross-examine witnesses.
5. A party can object to testimony or other evidence which is irrelevant, immaterial, or repetitious (however objections of the type used in a court of law will not be sustained).
6. Written testimony will be admitted in evidence at the hearing only if a witness cannot appear in person.
7. All testimony will be under oath.
8. Classified confidential information is not admittted.
9. Closing arguments from each party will be allowed.
10. The complaints examiner is empowered to:
    a. Administer oaths
    b. Regulate the course of the hearing
    c. Rule on evidence
    d. Rule on witnesses
    e. Exclude any person from the hearing for conduct that obstructs the hearing

Rights and Obligations of Opponents in an EEO Case

A. A defendant must abide by the following:
   1. The defendant is obligated to give the complaints examiner a list of those individuals he plans to call as witnesses at the hearing; he must also indicate what he expects each witness to establish.

2. The defendant (or his representative) has a right to be present throughout the hearing.
3. The defendant has a right to submit evidence in the form of exhibits, affidavits, or testimony of witnesses.
4. The defendant has a right to cross-examine the complainant's witnesses and introduce rebuttal evidence.

B. A complainant has the following rights:
1. The complainant can inspect the complaint file and all exhibits introduced at the hearing, and he must also be furnished with a copy of any exhibit that the defendant introduces at the hearing.
2. The complainant can refer to all matters relevant to the issues, but must avoid discussions of extraneous matters.
3. The complainant can request a delay or continuance of the case if fully justified.

Contents of an EEO Complaint File

The official EEO complaint file is usually available through a Freedom of Information request, and should contain the following:

1. A formal complaint
2. EEO counselor's report
3. A copy of the Notice of Receipt of the discrimination complaint as given to the complainant
4. The investigative file and affidavits of witnesses
5. A copy of the notice of the Proposed Disposition as given to the complainant
6. The complainant's written request for an EEO hearing
7. A copy of the written adjustment and the complainant's written request for reinstatement of the complaint
8. A copy of the administrative or judicial decision remanding the case to the agency for further processing after an agency's decision to reject or cancel the complaint

Checklist of Documents

Request the following documents in preparation for an EEO hearing:

1. Copies of complaint's efficiency ratings
2. All warning letters or negative evaluations of complainant's job performance, and the dates thereof

3. Complainant's official personnel file
4. EEO statistics for complainant's unit
5. Organization chart for agency in question
6. EEO affirmative-action plan for the agency, and date it was approved
7. All memoranda advertising positions in the agency at complainant's grade level or the level immediately above, during relevant time periods
8. All records of examinations offered or administered which would have provided upward mobility for the complainant
9. All grade scores of complainant which would qualify complainant for administrative positions
10. Copies of all agency personnel regulations concerning training

In the matter of (name of case)
the complaint of discrimination
filed by

_____
(complainant)

employed by _____
(agency)

at _____
(location of installation)

I _____ (name) _____

of _____ (address) _____

employed by _____ (name of agency) _____

at _____ (address) _____

answer the questions contained in this interrogatory so that it may be
entered in evidence in the record on the hearing in the matter of the
complaint referred to above.

First question:

Answer:

Second question:

Answer:

First cross-question:

Answer:

(continued)

Figure 21B–1. Sample Interrogatories in an EEO Case

Figure 21B–1 continued

Second cross-question:

Answer:

First question by the Complaints Examiner:

Answer:

This interrogatory must be sworn to, or affirmed, before a notary public or other person duly authorized to administer oaths or affirmations.

OATH

I _____(name)_____ solemnly swear that the answers I have given to the questions in this interrogatory are the truth, the whole truth, and nothing but the truth, so help me God.

_____

(signature)

AFFIRMATION

I _____solemnly affirm that the answers I have given to the questions in this interrogatory are the truth, and nothing but the truth.

_____

(signature)

Subscribed and sworn (affirmed) to before me this _____ day of _____19_____ .

SEAL   _____

(signature)

_____

(Printed name)

_____

(Authority to administer oath or affirmation)

From: EEO Counselor

To: Name of Person Counseled

Date:

This is to inform you that although counseling on the matter you brought to the attention of the EEO Counselor has not been completed, 21 calendar days have gone by since you first contacted the Counselor and you are now entitled, if you want to do so, to file a discrimination complaint if you believe you have been discriminated against on the basis of race, color, religion, sex or national origin.

If you do not file a complaint at this time, counseling will continue and your right to file a complaint will also continue until 15 calendar days AFTER THE FINAL INTERVIEW with the Counselor. The Counselor will inform you in writing when the final counseling interview is conducted.

If you file a complaint, it must be in writing and be filed in person or by mail with the <u>Director of Equal Employment Opportunity (provide specific mailing address)</u>, or any of the following officials authorized to receive discrimination complaints:

Agency Head

Installation Head

EEO Officer

Federal Woman's Program Coordinator

Figure 21B–2. Notice of Right to File an EEO Discrimination Complaint

From: EEO counselor

To: Name of Person Counseled

Date:

This is notice of the final counseling interview in connection with the matter you presented to the EEO Counselor.

If you believe you have been discriminated against on the basis of race, color, religion, sex or national origin, you have the right to file a COMPLAINT OF DISCRIMINATION WITHIN 15 CALENDAR DAYS AFTER RECEIPT OF THIS NOTICE.

The complaint must be in writing and may be filed in person or by mail with the Director of Equal Employment Opportunity (provide specific mailing address), or any of the following officials authorized to receive discrimination complaints:

Agency Head

Installation Head

EEO Officer

Federal Woman's Program Coordinator

Figure 21B–3. Sample Notice of Final Interview with EEO Counselor

Subject: Notice of Receipt of Discrimination Complaint

From: Director of EEO

To: Complainant

Date:

The purpose of this notice is to acknowledge receipt of your discrimination complaint and to provide you with written notification of your rights as well as the time requirements for exercising those rights. If you have further questions ask your EEO Counselor or Equal Employment Opportunity Officer.

Your complaint will be investigated. Based on the information developed by the investigation an effort at an adjustment on an informal basis will be made. You will receive a copy of the investigative report and have an opportunity to discuss it with an appropriate agency official.

If an adjustment of the complaint is arrived at, the terms of the adjustment will be reduced to writing and you will be provided a copy.

If an adjustment of the complaint is not arrived at, you will be notified in writing of the proposed disposition of the complaint. You will also be notified of your right to a hearing by an EEO Complaints Examiner who will recommend a decision to your agency or to a decision by the agency head or his designee without a hearing. If you want a hearing, or a decision by the agency head or his designee without a hearing, you must NOTIFY THE AGENCY IN WRITING WITHIN 15 CALENDAR DAYS OF RECEIPT OF THE PROPOSED DISPOSITION OF YOUR COMPLAINT.

(continued)

Figure 21B–4. Sample Notice of Receipt of Discrimination Complaint

Figure 21B–4 continued

If you fail to request a hearing or to ask for a decision by the agency head without a hearing within the 15 days of your receipt of the proposed disposition, that disposition will become the final decision of the agency. YOU MAY APPEAL THE FINAL AGENCY DECISION ON YOUR COMPLAINT TO THE COMMISSION WITHIN 15 CALENDAR DAYS OR YOU MAY FILE A CIVIL ACTION IN AN APPROPRIATE U.S. DISTRICT COURT WITHIN 30 DAYS.

If you are dissatisfied with the final decision of the agency (after a hearing or without a hearing), you may appeal to the Civil Service Commission within 15 calendar days of receipt of the notice or within 30 days you may file a civil action in an appropriate U.S. District Court.

If you decide to appeal to the Commission's Board of Appeals and Review you will still have an opportunity to file a civil action in U.S. District Court within 30 days after receipt of the Board's decision, or within 180 days of your appeal to the Board if no final decision has been rendered.

If the agency has not issued a final decision on your complaint within 180 days of the date it was filed, you may file a civil action in an appropriate U.S. District Court.

From: EEO Officer

To: Complainant

Date:

The purpose of this notice is to inform you of the proposed disposition of your discrimination complaint and your rights if you are dissatisfied with the proposed disposition.

PROPOSED DISPOSITION

(State the specific disposition of the complaint)

RIGHT OF HEARING

If you are dissatisfied with the proposed disposition, you may request a hearing and decision by the agency head or his designee, if YOU NOTIFY THE AGENCY WITHIN 15 CALENDAR DAYS OF RECEIPT OF THE NOTICE that you desire a hearing.

RIGHT OF DECISION WITHOUT A HEARING

If you are dissatisfied with the proposed disposition, you may request a decision by the head of the agency or his designee without a hearing.

If you fail to notify the agency of your wishes within the 15-day period, the EEO Officer may adopt as the agency's final decision the proposed disposition shown above and will so notify you in writing. Upon receipt of notification you may appeal to the Civil Service Commission within 15 calendar days or file a civil action in a Federal District Court within 30 days.

If you appeal to the Commission, you may still file a civil action within 30 days of receipt of the Commission decision or within 180 days of your appeal to the Commission if you have not received a final decision from the Commission.

Figure 21B–5. Sample Notice of Proposed Disposition of Discrimination Complaint

From: Agency Head or Designee

To: Complainant

Date:

Attached to this notice is the final decision of the agency on your complaint of discrimination. If you are dissatisfied with this final decision, you have the following appeal rights:

You may appeal to the Civil Service Commission within 15 calendar days of receipt of the decision.

You may file a civil action in an appropriate U.S. District Court within 30 days of receipt of the decision.

If you elect to appeal to the Commission, a civil action in a U.S. District Court may be filed within 30 days of receipt of the Commission's final decision.

A civil action may also be filed any time after 180 days of date of initial appeal to the Commission, if there has not been a final decision rendered.

Note to Agency:

This form is to be used under the following circumstances:

1. When a discrimination complaint is rejected or cancelled;

2. When a proposed disposition is adopted after failure to request a hearing or decision by the agency without a hearing;

3. When a final agency decision is made after a recommended decision by the Complaints Examiner; and

4. When an agency makes a final decision on the merits without a hearing.

A copy of the notice as given to the complainant should be filed by the agency in the complaint file.

Figure 21B–6. Sample Notice of EEO Final Decision

22 Who Regulates the Banks

A federal grand jury in Seattle is looking into a mobile-home lending scheme involving a bank and three mobile-home dealerships. The Federal Deposit Insurance Corporation assumed control of a bank with assets in excess of $700 million and deposits of more than $500 million. It also commenced a search for another bank to purchase the failed institution. Another financial institution faces charges that it lent its directors and their friends more than $50 million.

Banking is a powerful industry, with a diverse and powerful constituency. It is governed by a multiplicity of rules, regulations, and regulatory bodies that have proliferated in the last seventy years. The banking regulators vary in their needs, jurisdiction, power, and the rules and regulations they enforce.

Some of the regulators concern themselves solely with the country's national banks. Others have jurisdiction over the savings and loan institutions. Some are concerned with international financial transactions; others concentrate solely on the domestic. How and who regulates the financial institutions is the subject of this chapter.

Federal Reserve System (Fed)

Established in 1913 under the Federal Reserve Act, the Fed serves as the nation's central banker.[1] Its function is to regulate the country's monetary policy. The Fed also regulates state-chartered member banks.[2]

The Fed handles the federal government's deposits and debt issues, acting as a lender of last resort and handling the transfer of funds. In addition, through its regulatory powers the Fed serves to maintain the nation's commercial banking system.

The Fed's system consists of a number of key institutions, including the following.

A Board of Governors based in Washington, D.C.

Twelve Federal Reserve Banks and twenty-five branches and related facilities based around the country

A federal Open Market Committee

A federal Advisory Council

Its member commercial banks

The member banks include both national and state-chartered institutions.[3] Membership in the Fed is voluntary.

The Fed's board is composed of seven members. These are appointed by the President, with the advice and consent of the Senate. This group of men and women is responsible for determining the Fed's monetary, credit, and operating policies. The board is also responsible for formulating rules and regulations for the Fed's member banks. For example, it can:

Fix the requirements concerning reserves to be maintained by member banks.

Determine the maximum rate of interest that can be paid by members on their deposits.

Review and determine the discount rate charged by the Federal Reserve Banks.

Carry out examinations of the Federal Reserve Banks.

Supervise transactions between the Federal Reserve Banks and foreign banks.

Supervise the issuance and retirement of Federal Reserve notes.

The board can also authorize the admission and termination of state banks and trust companies into the Fed's system, as well as branching and mergers by these institutions. For example, the board can grant authority to member banks to establish foreign branches or invest in foreign banks; it can also establish minimum standards for security devices and procedures used by these institutions.

If the board were to uncover any unsafe or unsound practice by a member state bank, it could issue a cease and desist order. It is authorized to suspend any member bank that uses the Fed's credit facilities for speculative purposes.

The board is authorized, under the Bank Holding Company Act of 1956, to pass on bank acquisitions by holding companies.[4] The Truth-in-Lending Act authorizes the board to promulgate regulations that assure adequate disclosure by member banks of their credit terms.[5] In addition, the board regulates the issuance of credit cards and any liabilities connected to their unauthorized use.[6]

Although the board is an important component of the Fed, there are several other important entities. These are as follows.

1. *Federal Advisory Council (FAC):* it consists of twelve members; each is selected annually from one of the Fed's twelve Reserve Bank districts. The FAC acts as an advisory body in general business matters that fall within the Fed's jurisdiction; it meets at least four times a year in Washington.

2. *Federal Open Market Committee (FOMC);* its membership includes seven members of the Fed's board and five representatives from the Federal Reserve Banks; the latter are selected annually. The FOMC regulates: open-market operations of the Reserve Banks; transactions in foreign currencies; federal government obligations; and currency arrangements between the Fed and the other central banks.

3. *Federal Reserve Banks (FRBs):* there are twelve such banks, located in Boston, New York, Philadelphia, Cleveland, Richmond, Atlanta, Chicago, St. Louis, Minneapolis, Kansas City, Dallas, and San Francisco. Each of these banks has a nine-member board of directors. The directors are equally divided into three classes:

Class A: these directors come from the stockholding member banks.

Class B: these come from the business communities in the district of the FRBs. They may not be connected with any bank.

Class C: these cannot be officials, employees, or stockholders of any bank.

The first two classes are selected by the stockholding member banks; while the last class is selected by the Fed's board.

The board of each FRB selects a president who serves a five-year term. The appointment, however, must be approved by the Fed's board. The FRBs provide a number of services for their member banks. For example, they discount bank notes, drafts, and bills of exchange; and make advances to their member banks upon their promissary notes for periods not exceeding ninety days. The FRBs also issue Federal Reserve notes, and they are authorized to act as clearinghouses and collecting agents for their member banks. In addition, they act as depositories and fiscal agents of the federal government.

4. *Consumer Advisory Council (CAC):* CAC consists of twenty-eight members. The council's function is to advise the Fed's board on consumer-related legislation and policies.

The Fed has come under increasing attack in the last several years from both Congress and consumer advocates. They charge that the Fed is guided solely by the interests of its members; its defenders, in turn, are opposed to any changes in the Fed's structure or jurisdiction. Irrespective of one's views on this subject, the Fed is an important federal banking regulator.

Federal Deposit Insurance Corporation (FDIC)

Established as an independent government-owned corporation, the FDIC is managed by a three-member board.[7] One of the members is the Comptroller of the Currency; while the other two are presidential appointments. The members serve six-year terms.

The chief function of the corporation is to insure the funds of its member banks. The FDIC also acts as a regulator for those state-chartered banks that are not members of the Federal Reserve System. However, all national and state Fed member banks are automatically insured by the FDIC.

In its capacity as a regulator, the FDIC requires member banks to:

Undergo periodic examinations.

Provide information on their financial condition.

Obtain approval before relocating.

Obtain approval for mergers.

Abide by consumer legislation.

Report on changes in ownership.

Maintain an adequate security system to discourage robberies.

Abide by all FDIC rules and regulations.

FDIC examinations have two important functions: first, they seek to ensure that management complies with the FDIC's rules and regulations; and second, they serve to review a member bank's overall operations. The reviews include an examination of a bank's assets, capital, income, loan policies, loans to insiders, investment policies, and internal controls. All member banks are required to comply with these FDIC examinations.

Should the FDIC conclude that a member bank is either in poor financial condition or the victim of illegal acts by management, it is authorized to take the following steps.

Remove or suspend the officer or director in question

Terminate the member bank's insurance coverage

Explore less formal (voluntary) channels to resolve the problem

Institute formal proceedings (this involves a hearing before an administrative law judge)

Act as a receiver should the member bank become insolvent

The FDIC maintains a list of member banks that have serious financial problems; the list is not public.

The FDIC has, its critics charge, a poor record when it comes to looking out for the public's interest. It is, they note, a captive of its own member banks. It has occasionally closed its eyes to unsound banking practices, and even fraud, by management. Whether these charges have merit is a matter of dispute.

Federal Home Loan Bank Board (FHLBB)

The FHLBB was established by the Federal Home Loan Bank Act as an independent agency within the executive branch.[8] The agency is headed by a three-member board; its members are nominated by the President and confirmed by the Senate.

The FHLBB's activities are supported by twelve regional Federal Home Loan Banks and the Federal Home Loan Insurance Corporation. The capital stock of the Federal Home Loan Banks is owned by member institutions.

Not all financial institutions, however, are eligible for Federal Home Loan Bank membership. Only savings and loans institutions, savings and cooperative banks, insurance companies, and building and loan homestead associations qualify for membership. All federal and state-chartered savings and loan associations insured by the Federal Savings and Loan Insurance Corporation are required to become members of their regional Federal Home Loan Banks.

The FHLBB's jurisdiction is broad, and influences numerous facets of the savings and loan industry. Its responsibilities cover both the supervision and regulation of federal and state-chartered savings and loan associations. The FHLBB is also responsible for:[9]

Issuing charters.

Promulgating rules and regulations for the industry.

Supervising and examining its members.

Approving new federal savings and loan associations.

Within the FHLBB's structure are also housed the Federal Savings and Loan Insurance Corporation[10] and the Federal Savings and Loan Advisory Council. The latter consults and makes recommendations to the FHLBB regarding the Federal Home Loan Bank System.

The FHLBB's broad jurisdiction is based on many federal statutes. These are as follows.

1. Housing and Community Development Act
2. Home Mortgage Disclosure Act
3. Home Finance Act of 1970
4. Home Owner's Loan Act of 1933
5. National Housing Act of 1934
6. NOW Accounts Act
7. Electronic Funds Transfer Act
8. Open Housing Act of 1968
9. Truth-in-Lending Act
10. Federal Home Loan Bank Act
11. Fair Credit Reporting Act
12. Equal Credit Opportunity Act
13. Bank Protection Act
14. Fair Debt Collection Practices Act of 1977
15. Federal Trade Commission Act

Like most of the other bank regulators, the FHLBB has come under criticism. Charges have been made that it is a clone of the very industry that it was established to regulate. Irrespective of the charges, the fact remains that in the area of savings and loans, the FHLBB is an important institution.

National Credit Union Administration (NCUA)

The NCUA's function is to supervise and regulate the federal credit unions.[11] The NCUA administers the National Credit Union Share Insurance Funds, and is responsible for chartering and insuring its credit-union members.[12]

Although headquartered in Washington, the NCUA's supervisory and regulatory functions are carried out by its six regional offices. Authority is vested in a three-member body which is nominated by the President and confirmed by the Senate for six-year terms.

Unlike the banks, the NCUA-member credit unions are financial cooperatives. They are designed to encourage savings and provide low-cost credit to their members. They serve regional, occupational, and associational groups; only persons connected with one of these groups can become members.

Unlike the other financial institutions, credit unions are managed by boards and committees made up of their members. Earnings are returned to the members in the form of dividends. The NCUA charters only the federal credit unions, and membership in the NCUA is mandatory. Local credit unions, however, are chartered by their respective states; NCUA membership is optional.

Before a credit union will be granted a NCUA charter, it must comply with certain minimum guidelines. It must also agree to submit to periodic NCUA examinations. The examinations ensure compliance with the NCUA's rules and regulations, and also identify potential or existing problems. The NCUA is authorized to investigate complaints from the public when potential violations of federal consumer laws are involved.

Export–Import Bank (Eximbank)

Eximbank was first organized as a banking corporation,[13] and later became an independent agency under the Export–Import Bank Act. Its function is to assist in the financing of imports and exports, and also in the exchange of commodities between the United States and foreign nations.

The Eximbank is authorized to borrow from the U.S. Treasury and also to have capital stock. The bank also extends direct credit to borrowers outside the United States, and export credit insurance and guarantees. The Eximbank will only finance part of the export costs; the balance of the financing must be provided by the borrower from its own resources or private sources. The bank, can guarantee part or all of the private financing.

The bank's programs are designed primarily to assist American exports. Its financial guarantees, discounts, and loans are designed to minimize the financing risks of exporters and private banks. Eximbank, however, has come under criticism; it is charged that the thrust of its programs is directed at assisting large American companies doing business overseas. Little of its financial assistance is directed at the small exporters of goods and services.

Pension Benefit Guaranty Corporation (PBGC)

Title IV of the Employee Retirement Income Security Act of 1974 (ERISA) created the PBGC, and brought private pension and welfare plans under its regulatory control.[14] PBGC is a wholly owned federal corporation; subject to the provisions of the Government Corporation Control Act.[15]

The corporation is governed by a three-member board, which consists of the Secretaries of Commerce, Labor, and Treasury. The board is responsible for establishing guidelines and policies for the corporation; in turn, the board is assisted by a seven-member Advisory Committee. The committee's members are appointed by the President; two of these come from the labor sector, two from business, and three from government.

Title IV of ERISA requires the PBGC to create two pension-plan insurance programs, and to establish the terms of a third. These insurance programs are the:

1. Contingent Employer Liability. This program insures employers who maintain or contribute to pension plans covered by ERISA in the event that the plan terminates, or its assets are insufficient to cover its guaranteed basic benefits.
2. Basic Benefits. This program guarantees all nonforfeitable basic benefits, if the plan should terminate without sufficient assets.
3. Nonbasic Benefits. This PBGC is authorized to establish programs to guaranty payment of nonbasic plans.

In the event that a pension plan terminates, the PBGC will ensure that its assets are properly employed. The PBGC can also take over the plan and administer it, thus ensuring continuation of operation. To ensure compliance with its rules and regulations, the PBGC requires that member plans submit periodic reports. These are open to the public for inspection.

The financial regulators play an important role in the daily lives of the U.S. public. Their rules and regulations determine the cost of finances; and, in the case of the Fed, the very health of the U.S. economy.

Notes

1. See, 12 U.S.C. 635.
2. See, 12 U.S.C. 221.
3. Nationally chartered banks are regulated by the Comptroller of the Currency; state-chartered non-Fed member banks are regulated by the Federal Deposit Insurance Corporation.
4. See, 12 U.S.C. 1841.
5. See, 12 U.S.C. 1601.

6. The Fed's board also has rule-making authority for the: Home Mortgage Disclosure Act; Federal Trade Commission Act (as it applies to financial institutions only); Fair Credit Billing Act; and Equal Credit Opportunity Act.

7. See, 12 U.S.C. 1811–1831.

8. See, 12 U.S.C. 1421 et seq.

9. See, *Code of Federal Regulations,* Title XII, part 500.

10. See, 12 U.S.C. 1724 et seq.

11. See, 12 U.S.C. 1752.

12. See, *Code of Federal Regulations,* Title XII, part 720.

13. See, Executive Order 6581.

14. See, 29 U.S.C. 1301 et seq.

15. See, 31 U.S.C. 846.

Conclusion

The federal edifice has been compared to a Chinese puzzle. Finding one's way around Washington can often prove difficult. It occasionally eludes even the insider. Visit any federal agency in Washington and you will find its hallways cluttered with lawyers, lobbyists, and an army of consultants, ready to do battle for their clients and causes. Armed with a knowledge of this labyrinth, these men and women (elected by none) have come to enjoy a monopoly over our instruments of governance.

The Washington insider has become a de facto power broker. By simply knowing what doors to open, what agencies to contact, and who has jurisdiction over a particular problem, the insider commands both large fees and awe. Even many of the nation's largest and best-known corporations flock to the insider with their ills.

Take, for example, the case of a New England corporation that spent $400,000 on Washington counsel to represent it in an SEC investigation. Many of the services, as it turned out, were not necessary. Had its general counsel had a basic grasp of SEC investigations, he could have saved his company the money. There is also the case of the lobbyist who charged his client $10,000 to simply tell him what he could have discovered for himself, by making use of the FOIA and a postage stamp.

Washington is approachable. The public can make itself felt and have a voice in the process of governance. You need not abdicate your rights to the lobbyists, lawyers, and consultants. Even a labyrinth has its exits; with a little patience and guidance, you can find your way out.

When dealing with the federal edifice, there are some simple guidelines you should keep in mind. They are as follows.

1. Never be intimidated by Washington. It can easily awe the outsider, but it does so simply because he lacks an understanding of the process and the jurisdiction of the agencies. The federal bureaucracy thrives on the outsider's fears; it trades on our ignorance.

2. When dealing with Washington, make sure you know what you want, and how to find the agency or source that can do it; this book should prove of some value as regards the latter. By knowing what agency to contact, you have managed to surmount your first hurdle. That should enable you to save time and money.

3. When dealing with the federal bureaucracy, do not take "no" for an answer. When the bureaucrat tells you no, he really means that he does not know how to help you. You will find that the bureaucrat is a prisoner of his own maze. Be persistent. If one door is shut, then try the next one.

4. Remember that the telephone is a powerful tool. A call to an

agency's general counsel office or public information officer can help get you on the right track. Calling the agency's head may also help. If all else fails, turn to your Congressman. His staff can often direct you to the correct office.

5. Do not be intimidated by titles or the aura of power. You will be surprised to find how accessible Washington is. If need be, have your member of Congress write an introductory letter. Follow up with a telephone call. This will often serve to get your foot inside the office. Once in, be prepared to detail your case and be specific as to your request. Vague and general requests will often go unanswered.

6. Do not hesitate to use the FOIA to gain access to records and other information stored in an agency's files. Remember that anyone can place an FOIA request. The burden falls on the agency to justify its refusal of a request. The FOIA also provides for legal fees and court costs.

7. Stand up for your rights. Do not hesitate to use the Privacy Act to ensure that the records the bureaucracy maintains on you are accurate. The act also ensures that your privacy is safeguarded; it provides for fines and criminal sanctions against any bureaucrat who violates its provisions.

8. Remember that the Government in the Sunshine Act, the Federal Register, and the Code of Federal Regulations can also be employed to open the agencies to public scrutiny. The law mandates that agencies open their decision making to the public, and that they allow the public to comment on proposed rules and regulations. If used properly, these laws can help you open up the federal edifice.

9. The Congress, with its many committees and subcommittees, can often be a valuable resource. It is also a forum for changing the nation's laws. By understanding Congress, its needs, and how it functions, you will be able to have some form of input in the legislative process. Congress is often more responsive to public pressure than the executive branch.

10. Washington has been called a giant marketplace. It works through the process of give and take. Compromise and red tape are the norm. You will often be asked: "What can you do for me in return?" Be prepared to address that question. Also be ready to explain your position in easy-to-understand language. Be polite yet firm. Direct threats will get you nowhere. Persuasion, however, can take many forms; this will depend on the place and persons involved.

11. Remember that Washington belongs to the people. The bureaucracy and politicians occasionally forget this; armies of lobbyists, lawyers, and other suppliants help them forget. You, however, should be ready to wake them from their dream.

Power can enchant and tempt. Knowledge, however, can bring balance. When used properly by the public, knowledge can check an overzealous bureaucracy. An educated laity is the best guarantee that our institutions of governance will not become isolated from those they were created to serve. Making Washington work for you is not only possible, it is necessary. It can serve to ensure that our democracy will survive.

Appendixes

Appendix A
Federal Sources of
Information

Technical Sources

The federal bureaucracy can provide a wealth of data to researchers, professionals, and others on an array of economic matters.

Sources of Information on General Matters

Data Users Services Division
Bureau of Census Department of Commerce
Washington, D.C. 20233
(excellent source for census data)

U.S. International Trade Commission
701 E Street, N.W. Room 154
Washington, D.C. 20436
(data on international trade)

National Bureau of Standards
Department of Commerce
Washington, D.C. 20234
(technical data on most industries)

National Referral Center
Library of Congress
10 First Street, S.E.
Washington, D.C. 20540
(general information on all subjects)

Bureau of Labor Statistics
Department of Labor
441 G Street, N.W.
Washington, D.C. 20212
(labor statistics information)

Federal Information Center
General Services Administration
7th & D Streets, S.W., Room 5716
Washington, D.C. 20407
(general information on government)

Patent Office
Department of Commerce
2021 Jefferson Davis Highway
Building 3, Crystal Plaza
Arlington, VA 22202
(information related to patents)

Federal Trade Commission
6th & Pennsylvania Avenue, N.W., Room 130
Washington, D.C. 20580
(information on major corporations)

Sources of Information on the Energy Industry

Office of Public Affairs
Department of Energy
Washington, D.C. 20585

National Energy Information Center
Department of Energy
1726 M Street, N.W., Room 230
Washington, D.C. 20461

National Solar Heating and Cooling Information Center
P.O. Box 1607
Rockville, MD 20850

Reference Branch
Technical Information Center
Department of Energy
P.O. Box 62
Oak Ridge, TN 37830

Office of Energy Conservation
National Bureau of Standards
Department of Commerce
Gaithersburg, MD 20234

Energy and Minerals Division
General Accounting Office
Room 5120
441 G Street, N.W.
Washington, D.C. 20548

Energy and Environment Division
Department of Transportation
400 7th Street, S.W., Room 4102
Washington, D.C. 20590

Energy and Science Division
Office of Management and Budget
Room 8001
New Executive Office Building
Washington, D.C. 20503

Fuels and Energy Office
Department of State
Room 3524A
22nd & C Streets, N.W.
Washington, D.C. 20520

International Energy Policy
Department of Treasury
Room 4134
15th & Pennsylvania Avenue, N.W.
Washington, D.C. 20220

Nuclear Energy and Technological Affairs
Department of State
Room 7830
Washington, D.C. 20520

Energy Systems Division
National Aeronautics and Space Administration
Code R–14
600 Independence Avenue, S.W.
Washington, D.C. 20546

Energy and Mineral Technology Coordination
Bureau of Mines
2401 E Street, N.W. Room 1005
Washington, D.C. 20241

The Government Printing Office As a Source

The Government Printing Office (GPO) carries many government publications that can be of value to you. For instructions on how to order a book, or for a catalogue, contact the nearest GPO office. GPO offices are located in the following cities.

Washington, D.C.: 710 N. Capitol St.; Commerce Department, 14th & E N.W.; Forrestal Bldg., 1000 Independence Ave. S.W.; Pentagon Building; Main Concourse; State Department, 21st & C N.W.; USIA, 1776 Pennsylvania Ave. N.W.

Atlanta, GA.: Federal Office Bldg., 275 Peachtree N.E. (30303)

Birmingham, AL.: 2121 8th Ave. N. (35203)

Boston, MA.: John F. Kennedy Federal Bldg. (02115)

Canton, OH.: 201 Cleveland Ave., S.W. (44702)

Chicago, IL: Federal Office Bldg., 219 S. Dearborn St. (60604)

Cleveland, OH.: Federal Bldg., 1240 E. 9th St. (44114)

Dallas, TX.: New Federal Bldg., 1100 Commerce St. (75242)

Denver, CO.: Federal Bldg., and U.S. Courthouse, 1961 Stout St. (80202)

Detroit, MI.: Federal Office Bldg., 231 W. LaFayette Blvd. (48226)

Kansas City, MO.: Federal Bldg., 601 E. 12th St. (64106)

Los Angeles, CA.: Federal Bldg., 300 N. Los Angeles St. (90012)

New York, NY.: Federal Office Bldg., 26 Federal Plaza (10278)

Philadelphia, PA.: U.S. Post Office and Courthouse, 9th & Chestnut Sts. (91907)

San Francisco, CA.: Federal Bldg., 450 Golden Gate Ave., P.O. Box 36104 (94102)

Federal Contracting Sources

Government contracts are a multibillion-dollar annual industry. The federal government is the biggest consumer in the country. The following agencies and departments can supply you with information on the status and availability of government contracts.

Division of Installations and Logistics
Department of Transportation
400 7th Street, S.W.
Mail Stop M–60
Washington, D.C. 20590

Cost Review and Policy Branch
Environmental Protection Agency
PM214C
Crystal Mall Bldg., #2, Room 711
Washington, D.C. 20460

Division of Management Information Services
Department of Health, Education, and Welfare
330 Independence Avenue, S.W., Room 1076
Washington, D.C. 20201

Information Sources on Regulated Industries

Few if any industries have escaped the watchful eye of Washington's bureaucracy. The following agencies are excellent sources for information on regulated industries.

Industry	*Agency*
All Air Travel and Transport	Civil Aeronautics Board 1025 Connecticut Avenue, N.W. Washington, D.C. 20428
	Federal Aviation Administration 800 Independence Avenue, S.W. Washington, D.C. 20591
Banking	Board of Governors of the Federal Reserve System 20th & Constitution Avenue, N.W. Room B1122 Washington, D.C. 20551
	Controller of the Currency 4700 L'Enfant Plaza, East, S.W. Washington, D.C. 20219
Shipping and Barges	Federal Maritime Commission 1100 L Street, N.W. Washington, D.C. 20573
Educational Institutions	National Center for Educational Statistics 400 Maryland Avenue, S.W. Washington, D.C. 20202

Traders, Operators, and Merchants	Commodity Futures Trading Commission 1111 L Street, N.W. Washington, D.C. 20581
Consumer Products	Consumer Product Safety Commission 1111 L Street, N.W. Washington, D.C. 20207
Utilities (nonnuclear)	Federal Energy Regulatory Commission Department of Energy 825 North Capitol Street, N.E. Washington, D.C. 20426
Exporters	American International Traders Register Office of International Marketing U.S. Department of Commerce Washington, D.C. 20230
Federal Contractors	The Renegotiation Board 2000 M Street, N.W. Washington, D.C. 20446
Domestic Business	World Traders Data Reports Department of Commerce Washington, D.C. 20230
Hospital-Related Business	National Center for Health Statistics 5600 Fishers Lane Rockville, MD 20852
Real-Estate Developers	Office of Interstate Land Sales Registration Department of Housing and Development 451 17th Street, S.W., Room 4130 Washington, D.C. 20411

Mining Companies	Mine Safety and Health Administration Department of Interior 4015 Wilson Blvd. Arlington, VA 22203
Nuclear-Related Business	Nuclear Regulatory Commission Washington, D.C. 20555
Union Pension Plans	Department of Labor 200 Constitution Avenue, N.W. Washington, D.C. 20216
Pharmaceutical-Related Business	Food and Drug Administration 5600 Fishers Lane Rockville, MD 20852
Chemical Firms	Environmental Protection Agency 401 M Street, S.W. Washington, D.C. 20460
Publicly Held Companies	Securities and Exchange Commission 1100 L Street, N.W., Room 6101 Washington, D.C. 20549
Television Industry (also cable)	Federal Communications Commission 2025 M Street, N.W. Washington, D.C. 20554
Railroads, Trucking, Bus Lines, Freight Forwarders, Water Carriers, Oil Pipelines, and other transport-related activities	Interstate Commerce Commission 12th & Constitution Avenue, N.W. Washington, D.C. 20423
Federally Insured Savings and Loans Associations	Federal Home Loan Bank Board 1700 G Street, N.W. Washington, D.C. 20552
Telephone and Telegraph Companies	Federal Communications Commission 1919 M Street, N.W. Washington, D.C. 20554

Sources on International Markets

The federal bureaucracy is an excellent source of information for those who are interested in doing business overseas.

Government Agencies

U.S. Department of Interior
Bureau of Mines
International Division
2402 E Street, N.W.
Washington, D.C. 20241
(provides data on mineral resources)

U.S. Department of Agriculture
ESCS/Foreign Demand and Competition Division
500 12th Street, S.W.
Washington, D.C. 20250
(provides data on agricultural activities)

Agency for International Development
320 21st Street, N.W.
Washington, D.C. 20523
(deals with economic assistance to foreign countries)

Office of International Marketing
U.S. Department of Commerce
Room 4015B
Washington, D.C. 20230
(specialized information on specific countries)

U.S. Department of State
2201 C Street, N.W.
Washington, D.C. 20520
(general information on the political, economic, and cultural affairs of a foreign country)

U.S. Department of Energy
International Affairs
2000 M Street, N.W.
Washington, D.C. 20461
(specializes in foreign energy resources)

Publications

> *Global Market Surveys*
> (U.S. Department of Commerce)
>
> *Index to Foreign Market Reports*
> (U.S. Department of Commerce)
>
> *World Traders Data Report*
> (U.S. Department of Commerce)
>
> *New Product Information Service*
> (U.S. Department of Commerce)

General Sources

> International Population Division
> Bureau of Census
> Department of Commerce
> Washington, D.C. 20233
>
> Inter-American Development Bank
> 808 17th Street, N.W.
> Washington, D.C. 20577
>
> International Monetary Fund
> 700 19th Street, N.W.
> Washington, D.C. 20431
>
> World Bank
> 1818 H Street, N.W.
> Washington, D.C. 20433
>
> International Economics
> Bureau of Economic Analysis
> U.S. Department of Commerce
> Washington, D.C. 20230
>
> Office of Assistant Secretary for International Affairs
> Department of Treasury
> Washington, D.C. 20220
>
> European Community Information Service
> 2100 M Street, N.W., Suite 707
> Washington, D.C. 20037

Appendix B
Statutes under
which Plaintiffs Can
Recover Fees

There are dozens of federal statutes that provide for counsel fees for plaintiffs who prevail in litigation against the government; some of these, however, leave the award of fees to the discretion of the courts. The more important of these statutes are as follows.

Noise Control Act, 42 U.S.C. 4911(d)

Energy Policy and Conservation Act, 42 U.S.C. 6305(d)

Solid Waste Disposal Act, 42 U.S.C. 6972(e)

Clean Air Act, 42 U.S.C. 7413(b), 7604(d), and 7606(f)

Ocean Thermal Energy Conversion Act of 1980, 42 U.S.C. 9124(d)

Outer Continental Shelf Lands Act, 43 U.S.C. 1349(a) (5)

Natural Gas Pipeline Safety Act, 49 U.S.C. 1686(e)

Foreign Intelligence Surveillance Act of 1978, 50 U.S.C. 1810

Ethics in Government Act, 2 U.S.C. 288i(d)

Federal Contested Election Act, 2 U.S.C. 396

Freedom of Information Act, 5 U.S.C. 552(a) (4) (E)

Privacy Act, 5 U.S.C. 552a(g) (3) (B) and 552a(g) (4)

Government in the Sunshine Act, 5 U.S.C. 552b(1)

Civil Service Reform Act of 1978, 5 U.S.C. 5596(b) and 7701(g)

Right to Financial Privacy Act of 1978, 12 U.S.C. 3417(a) and 3418

Consumer Product Safety Act, 15 U.S.C. 2059(e)(4) and 2060(c)

Toxic Substances Control Act, 15 U.S.C. 2618(d), 2619(c)(2), and 2620(b) (4) (C)

Deep Seabed Hard Mineral Resources Act, 30 U.S.C. 1427(c)

Deepwater Ports Act, 33 U.S.C. 1515(d)

Safe Drinking Water Act 42 U.S.C. 300–8(d)

Civil Rights Attorney's Fees Awards Act of 1976, 42 U.S.C. 1988

Civil Rights of Institutionalized Persons Act, 42 U.S.C. 1997a and 1997c

Civil Rights Act of 1964, Title II, 42 U.S.C. 2000a–3(b)

Civil Rights Act of 1964, Title III, 42 U.S.C. 2000b–1

Civil Rights Act of 1964, Title VII, 42 U.S.C. 2000e–5(k)

Privacy Protection Act of 1980, 42 U.S.C. 2000aa–6

Legal Services Corporation Act, 41 U.S.C. 2996e

Uniform Relocation Assistance and Real Property Acquisition Policies Act, 42 U.S.C. 4654

Endangered Species Act, 16 U.S.C. 1540(g) (4)

Tax Reform Act of 1976, 26 U.S.C. 6110(i) (2)

Rehabilitation Act of 1973, 29 U.S.C. 794a

Black Lung Benefits Act, 30 U.S.C. 932(a)

Surface Mining Control and Reclamation Act, 30 U.S.C. 1270(d) and 1275(e)

State and Local Fiscal Assistance Amendments of 1976, 31 U.S.C. 12440(e)

Water Pollution Prevention and Control Act, 33 U.S.C. 1365(d)

Marine Protection, Research, and Sanctuaries Act, 33 U.S.C. 1415(g) (4)

Index

About the Author

August Bequai holds the L.L.M. from The George Washington University National Law Center, the J.D. from The American University, and the M.A. and B.A. from New York University. He is presently in the private practice of law in Washington. A former chairman of the Federal Bar Association's Subcommittee on White Collar Crime, he has also served as the vice-chairman of the Washington Bar's Committee of Regulatory Agencies. The author also sits on the Advisory Board of the *Journal of Media Law and Practice,* and has taught as an adjunct professor at The George Washington University and The American University. He has published extensively on various aspects of the law; his books are: *Computer Crime* (Lexington Books, D.C. Heath, 1977), *White Collar Crime: A Twentieth Century Crisis* (Lexington Books, D.C. Heath, 1978), *Organized Crime: The Fifth Estate* (Lexington Books, D.C. Heath, 1979), *Cashless Society: EFTS at the Crossroads* (1981), and *How to Prevent Computer Crime: A Guide for Managers* (1983).